the NATURE ACTIVITY BOOK

99 Ideas for Activities in the Natural World of Aotearoa New Zealand

RACHEL HAYDON
Illustrated by PIPPA KEEL

TE PAPA
PRESS

**THIS BOOK BELONGS TO
HE PUKAPUKA TĒNEI NĀ**

Ingoa | Name:

_____

Tau | Age:

_____

CONTENTS

SHAPES AND PATTERNS
9

ENVIRONMENT AND SPACES
41

EXPERIMENTS AND ENQUIRY
69

SENSE AND MINDFULNESS
101

ACTION AND KAITIAKITANGA
131

Finding out more
167

Glossary
168

Thank you
173

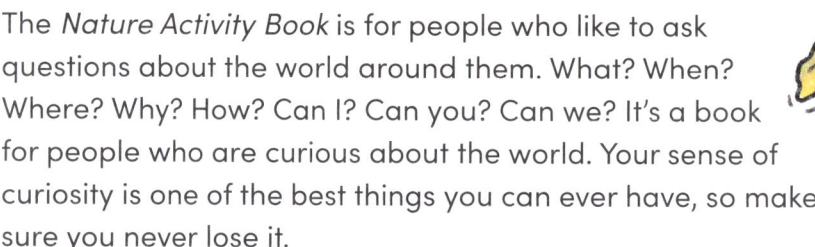

ABOUT THIS BOOK

Do you love to have fun and discover things?
Are you a waewae kai kapua – an adventurer?
Do you love to get outside into nature?

The *Nature Activity Book* is for people who like to ask questions about the world around them. What? When? Where? Why? How? Can I? Can you? Can we? It's a book for people who are curious about the world. Your sense of curiosity is one of the best things you can ever have, so make sure you never lose it.

It's also a book for young New Zealanders who like adventures, and who like to take friends and whānau along to share those adventures. You can explore the ideas and do the activities in this book by yourself, but they can be shared, too. Can a brother, sister or friend help you do something or go with you?

The pages ahead will encourage you to look closely at the things around you. What can you see? What are you feeling? How is everything connected? What can you build? What can you grow? How can *you* make something better for the people around you or for the planet? How can *we* make things better together?

This book will help you to ask great questions like: Why is that flower so beautiful? Why does the spider in the corner of my room have exactly eight legs? What are ocean waves? You may experience mīharo (awe and wonder) when you are out and about in nature. You will begin to really look, watch and see, and most importantly, you will want to share.

Take a look at the Materials section on the opposite page before you start. If you don't understand any of the words used in an activity, go to the Glossary on page 168. Websites that can give you more information are listed on page 171.

So, go for it! The world needs more waewae kai kapua like you. Use this book to keep track of your adventures so you can look back on what you've done and encourage others to be like you.

MATERIALS

The most important thing you'll need for the activities in this book is yourself, your sense of curiosity, and some adventurous friends and whānau to share the journey.

Here are some of the materials used for the activities in this book. Most can be found around the house and on your adventures, and it's OK if you don't have everything on this list – if you need to you can improvise or find alternatives that work for you. When you use some of the things listed here – like scissors, or a knife and a chopping board – you may need the help of an adult. Make sure you ask for help when you need it. When you are an adventurer, you have to make sure you do things safely.

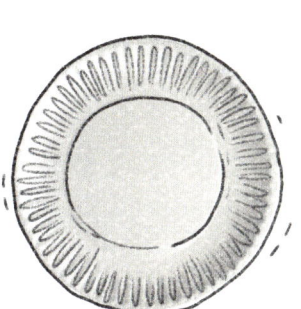

ART & CRAFT

- Pens and pencils
- Coloured markers, coloured pencils, crayons
- Paint and paintbrushes
- Black paper
- Chalk
- String, twine, nylon, thin rope
- Scissors
- Pinking shears (you can find these zigzag scissors at any fabric or sewing store)
- Ruler
- Tape measure
- Clear tape
- Duct tape
- Glue
- Exterior PVA glue
- Stapler and staples
- Nails
- Hammer
- Thumbtacks
- Wire
- Bamboo skewers
- Clear contact paper (self-adhesive book covering)
- Paper plates
- Paper straw
- Cloth bag (can just be a carry bag)
- A sewing pin
- Modelling clay (or Blu-Tack® will do)
- Small tiles (like mosaic tiles)
- 100% cotton – choose fabric in a design you like
- Spray bottle
- Sponge
- Two identical picture frames – just the frame, no backing or glass etc.
- Fine mesh or netting

FROM NATURE

- Leaves
- Flowers
- Rocks (pumice, limestone, river stones), pebbles, sand
- Pieces of quartz
- Shells
- Various fruits, herbs and vegetables: blackberries, red cabbage, spinach or mint leaves, bay leaves, turmeric, celery, celery leaves, carrots, onion skins, orange, berries, avocado skins, beetroot
- Seeds from fresh apples, tomatoes, chillies, capsicums or beans
- Tea leaves, coffee grinds
- Walnut shells
- Ivy, grape vine, willow, supplejack vines
- Potting mix or soil
- Plants or seedlings
- Various native plants
- Sticks or driftwood
- 'Compostable material' – leaves, grass, shredded newspaper, spoiled food waste (like fruit and vegetables)

RECYCLED MATERIALS

- Old clothing – shirt, T-shirt
- Old sheets, towels or tea towels
- Old wool/acrylic/polyester blanket
- Used newspaper
- Used paper (preferably used computer paper)
- Old cardboard
- Empty toilet paper tubes or paper towel rolls
- Glasses, jars or small containers
- Glass jars with lids
- Plastic jar with screw-top lid
- Empty clear, 2-litre plastic bottles
- Old cans (make sure the edges are not sharp)
- Big yoghurt containers

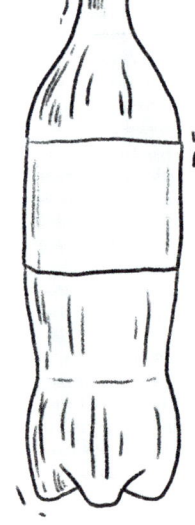

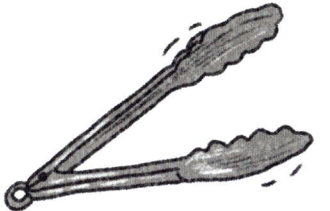

FROM THE KITCHEN

- Chopping board and a knife (and maybe the help of a grown-up!)
- Tongs
- Plate or shallow dish
- Spoon
- Vase, glass or tall container
- Large bowl
- Baking tray
- Baking paper
- Oven
- Large tub or sink
- Blender

BITS AND BOBS

- An iron and ironing board
- Hand lens or magnifying glass
- Navigation compass
- Coins (copper if possible)
- Piece of glass
- Steel nail
- Small spade
- At least 20–30 lengths of thin bamboo (about 4–5mm across in diameter)
- Jojoba oil*
- Organic beeswax pellets*
- Powdered food-grade pine rosin*
- Lots of heavy books
- Gardening or rubber gloves
- Camera (or camera phone) and printer

FOOD ITEMS

- Pasta tubes or shapes (that can be threaded onto string)
- Rice, dried beans, lentils
- Sunflower seeds (hulls still on)
- White millet (found in supermarkets, or you could use barley, quinoa or bulgur wheat)
- Honey
- Stale bread
- Shelled peanuts
- Cracked corn
- Popcorn
- Dried fruit – raisins, currants, sultanas
- Food colouring (red, blue or yellow)

* These can be bought through websites like www.purenature.co.nz

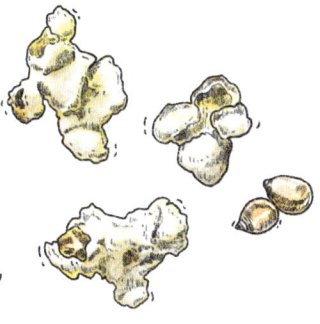

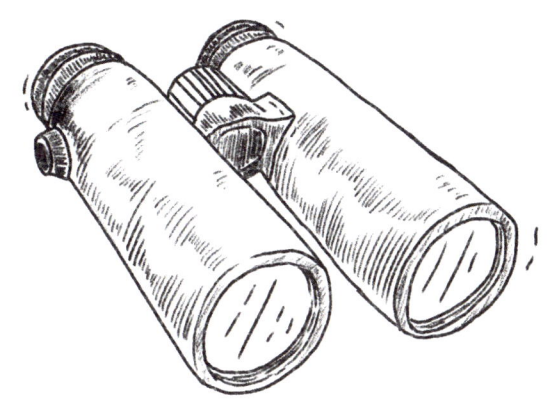

SHAPES AND PATTERNS

WHAT IS YOUR FAVOURITE SHAPE OR PATTERN IN NATURE?

Draw your favourite shape or pattern in nature here, or photograph it and then attach the photo to this page.

IDEAS
Think about the swirl on a shell, the hexagons of a honeycomb, ripples in sand, spider webs, spots on a ladybird, veins on a leaf or the koru of a silver fern.

Write down why you like this pattern.

_____
_____
_____
_____
_____
_____

NATURE TAKING SHAPE

Find as many shapes around you as you can.

Play 'I spy' with two-dimensional (2D) shapes: *'I spy a circle.'* (Is it the centre of a daisy?)

Make the game more challenging by using three-dimensional (3D) shapes: *'I spy a sphere.'* (Is it an orange?)

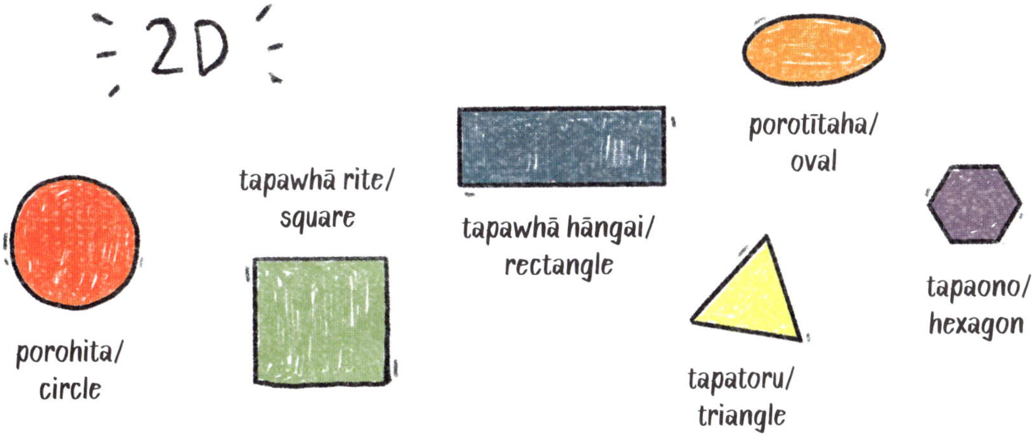

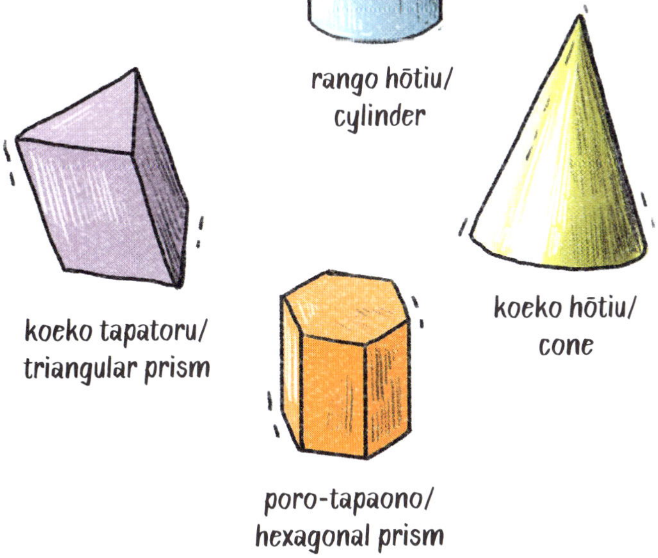

2D

- porohita/circle
- tapawhā rite/square
- tapawhā hāngai/rectangle
- porotītaha/oval
- tapatoru/triangle
- tapaono/hexagon

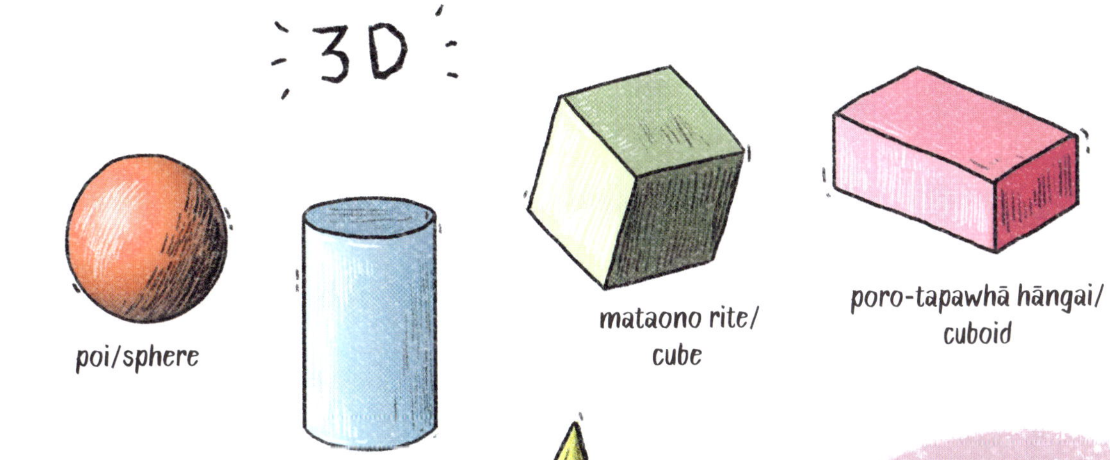

3D

- poi/sphere
- rango hōtiu/cylinder
- mataono rite/cube
- poro-tapawhā hāngai/cuboid
- koeko tapatoru/triangular prism
- poro-tapaono/hexagonal prism
- koeko hōtiu/cone

TIP

If you are playing with a younger friend or family member, help them to find these shapes with you. Teaching young children to identify shapes helps them recognise different letters and words, which supports their reading and writing.

COLLECT!

LEAF TYPES

Have you ever noticed how many different shapes of leaves there are? There are lots!

Try to find one of each of these leaf shapes and stick them here.

FAN-SHAPED

Like part of a necklace fern or frond

OVATE

Oval-shaped (the typical 'leaf' shape), like a northern rātā leaf

CORDATE

Heart-shaped, like a kawakawa leaf

LINEAR

Long and straight, like the leaves of a miro tree

PALMATIFID

Star-shaped, like a five-finger leaf

DELTOID

Triangle-shaped, like New Zealand spinach, or kōkihi

LANCEOLATE

Thin and stretched out, like a tawa leaf

LOBED

Shaped like lots of earlobes, such as a toatoa leaf

FLOWER TYPES

There are also many different shapes of flowers.

Try to find one of each of the flower shapes below. Lie them between two sheets of baking paper and place a very heavy book on top. Leave for two to three weeks to dry, then stick them onto this page.

NUMERIC
Usually with three to six petals arranged in a circle in a symmetrical pattern, like a poroporo flower or a geranium

CUP-SHAPED
Cup-shaped, like a buttercup or a poppy

DOME
Ball-shaped, like a dandelion head

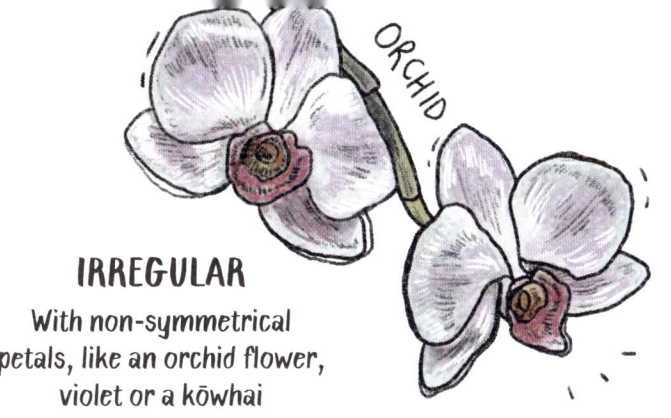

IRREGULAR
With non-symmetrical petals, like an orchid flower, violet or a kōwhai

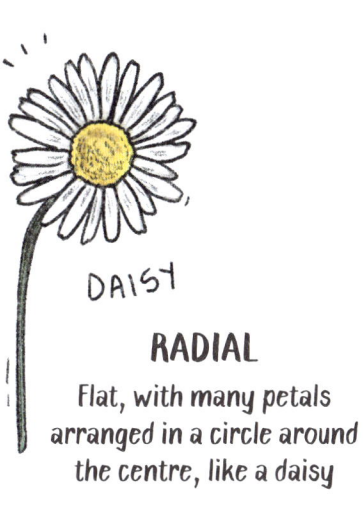

RADIAL
Flat, with many petals arranged in a circle around the centre, like a daisy

TRUMPET
Trumpet-shaped, like a daffodil or a petunia

SYMMETRY IN NATURE

There are four basic types of symmetry in nature and they are all shown here.

Try to find and draw examples of each of them.

REFLECTION

If you draw a line down the middle of the shape, it is the same on both sides, as in a butterfly or a crab

ROTATIONAL
The shape has similar parts arranged around a middle point, as in a snowflake or a starfish

each leaf pair is the same!

TRANSLATIONAL
The shape moves or can be repeated in a direction without changing shape, as in repeated pairs of leaves on a stem or a honeycomb

SPIRAL
The shape gradually widens (or tightens) from a middle point, as in an aloe leaf rosette or a nautilus shell

WATERY REFLECTIONS

Look at the reflections on very still water, such as the water in a glass or bowl, a puddle, a pond or a lake.

What does the reflection look like in the water? Is it perfect? Or is it wavy?

_____
_____

Why do you think the reflection looks this way?

_____
_____
_____
_____
_____
_____

On the opposite page, make a drawing of what you can see.

draw here!

PATTERNS IN SOUND

Listen . . . Can you identify any patterns in the sounds around you? In a call made by a bird? In the drip drip drip of a leaky tap?

Is the pattern fast or slow? Describe them all here.

_____
_____
_____
_____
_____
_____
_____
_____
_____

Can you draw a pattern that represents the sound you hear? Use the space below for your drawing.

PATTERNS OVER TIME

Have you noticed any patterns over time? Think about whether flowers are always in bloom, if there is a time of year when you can eat your favourite fruit, or what meals you eat every day. List some of them here.

_____
_____
_____

What patterns can you see in a day? A week? A month? A year? Below is an example to start you off. List some more patterns here.

1. The shape of the moon over a month
2. _____
3. _____
4. _____
5. _____
6. _____

MAKING ORDER OUT OF CHAOS

1. Collect a number of items (these can be anything at all). Draw and label them here.

2. Now, try to separate your items into groups according to one of the features they have in common, such as their size, the material they are made of, their colour or their shape. How have you grouped them?

   Draw and label your groupings here.

3. Try to group your items in another two different ways. Draw them here.

4. In science, this is called 'classification'. It is an important way to group living things according to their similarities. In order for scientists around the world to agree on how things are classified, what do you think needs to happen first? (See answer below if you're stuck.)

_____
_____
_____
_____
_____
_____
_____
_____
_____

Answer: They would all need to agree on which features are used to classify living things. If they didn't, how would a scientist in Japan and a scientist in New Zealand know they were talking about exactly the same type of fruit fly or same type of grass?

CLASSIFYING WILDLIFE

Match each of the animals pictured with their name in the following list: moko/Otago skink, kea, kiwi, pūwhaiau/gurnard, waiaua/Hector's dolphin, kōura, wētā, pekapeka/short-tailed bat, kekeno/New Zealand fur seal, kororā/little blue penguin, tuatara.

How many ways can you group these animals? By size? By colour? By their body coverings?

Write about your groupings here.

_____
_____
_____
_____
_____
_____
_____
_____

MINIBEAST TREASURE HUNT

A minibeast is a commonly found animal that scientists call an *invertebrate*. These animals have their skeletons on the outsides of their bodies, in the form of a shell or hard outer layer. Some minibeasts like earthworms don't have a skeleton at all.

Below, there are five different types of minibeast. Find one of each of these types of minibeast in a garden, a park or wherever you are out and about. When you do, write its name or draw a picture of it in the correct box.

MYRIAPODS

Their name means '10,000 feet'. Their body is made up of many similar sections, most of which have jointed legs. Myriapods include millipedes and centipedes.

CENTIPEDE

ARACHNIDS

Their name comes from the Greek word for spider. Their body is made up of two sections, and they have four pairs of legs (eight altogether) and no antennae. Arachnids include spiders, scorpions, mites and ticks.

NZ HOUSE SPIDER

INSECTS

Their name means 'with a divided body'. Their body is made up of three sections, and they have three pairs of legs (six altogether) and usually one or two pairs of wings. Insects include beetles, wasps and bees.

HONEY BEE

MOLLUSCS

Their name means 'soft'. They have a soft, unsegmented body that is usually surrounded by a shell. Molluscs include snails, clams and squid.

CLAM/PIPI

CRUSTACEANS

Their name means 'crust'. They have a hard outer shell (the 'crust') with a pair of legs on each segment, and two pairs of antennae. Crustaceans include lobsters, crabs and woodlice.

WOODLOUSE

MAKE!

CREATE A NATURE SCAVENGER HUNT

A scavenger hunt is a game where you have to find a number of different objects. Take all the ideas you have explored in this section so far – leaf shapes, flower shapes, types of minibeast and so on – and create a list of twelve things for your friends and whānau to find. Tell the scavenger hunters to simply tick each thing off the list when they find it. They could also take a photo if they want to. You could give them a few hours or a few days to do this.

1.
2.
3.
4.
5.
6.
7.
8.
9.
10.
11.
12.

CLOSE-UPS

Look at a small plant or animal through a hand lens or magnifying glass. Can you see any patterns on it?

Look at the close-ups of patterns below. What objects do you think they are found on? A leaf? A butterfly's wing? A shell? Record your answers under each picture. Think about how you made your decision, or 'conclusion'.

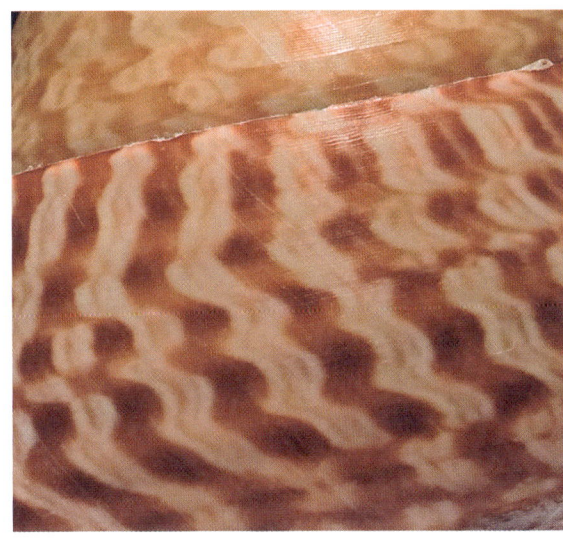

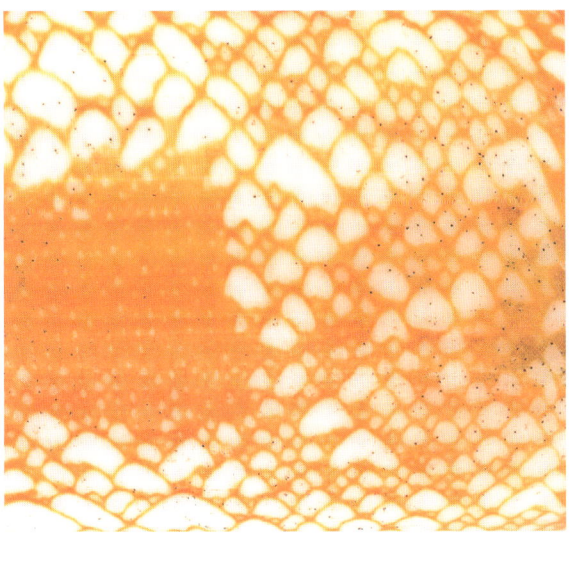

Answer: Butterfly, shell, shell, leaf.

FOOD CHAINS

A food chain shows connections between living things by linking what eats what.

For example, the soil in your garden contains plant material that is eaten by worms, which in turn are eaten by birds, which themselves are eaten by cats. Think about the plants and animals that live in your local area, or 'environment', and the links that join them together in food chains (think about what eats what!). Can you come up with five food chains? Draw them in the boxes provided.

CHALLENGE

Can you find ways these chains interconnect to make a food web? This is where multiple food chains link together to make a much larger web. For example, the worm above may also be eaten by a rat, which is eaten by a cat, and the cat also eats birds!

A YEAR OF CHANGE

Find a spot in nature that you love to look at – any scene will do, so long as it's important to you. Take a photo of it and make a note of exactly where you took your photo from. Glue or tape your photo to this page.

Take a photo of the same scene from the same spot after three months, then after another three months, and then another three months. How has the scene changed over the year? What do you think has caused it to change? If you can, attach print-outs of your photos to these pages.

PHOTO #1

Place:

Date:

PHOTO #2

Place:

Date:

PHOTO #3

Place:

Date:

PHOTO #4

Place:

Date:

FORCES IN NATURE

A 'force' is a push or pull upon an object that is caused by its interaction with another object.

Many things within nature are shaped by natural forces. For example, can you find:

- ☐ A rock shaped by water
- ☐ The ground shaped by an animal
- ☐ A shell shaped by an animal
- ☐ A tree shaped by wind
- ☐ A leaf shaped by an animal

Draw the objects you found here or attach a photo of any of them.

MAKE!

BOUNTIFUL BUNTING

As autumn begins, leaves fall from deciduous trees – these are the trees that lose their leaves every year. Evergreen trees have leaves that stay green all year, even once they have fallen. Collect fallen leaves and use them to create beautiful bunting to decorate a space of your choice.

MATERIALS

- Scissors  
- Tape or glue
- String 
- Selection of autumn leaves in different shapes, colours and sizes

WHAT TO DO:

1. Using scissors, cut the string to the length you want your bunting to be.
2. Use the tape or glue to attach the leaves to the string. Alternatively, you could pierce a hole in each leaf and thread them onto the string, leaving a gap of 10cm or so between the leaves.
3. Tie up your bunting at each end.

CHALLENGE

Try to use leaves from deciduous trees that are native to Aotearoa New Zealand – those that grow here naturally and haven't arrived from somewhere else. There are only twenty-eight tree species in all of Aotearoa New Zealand that are deciduous!

POUWHENUA
– A STORY AND PATTERN OF PLACE

Pouwhenua are carved wooden posts used by Māori to mark boundaries or places of importance. Pouwhenua tell a story. Their carvings tell of the connection between ancestors, of the environment and of the character of the tangata whenua, the local people.

Is there a pouwhenua in your local area? Can you guess its story from what you can see? If not, how can you find this out?

Draw the pouwhenua here, or write the story it represents, below.

Now create a design for a pouwhenua of your own that tells a story of your whānau. It could include drawings of your family members, your house and a local landmark, or even a pet.

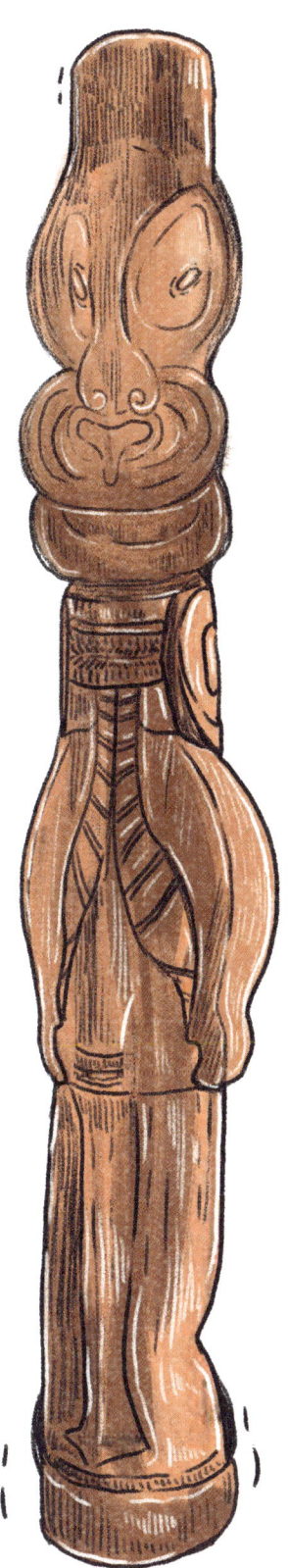

MAKE!

RANGOLI PATTERNS

Rangoli patterns originated in India, Nepal and Bangladesh. These beautiful decorations are said to bring good luck. The patterns are symmetrical and are traditionally drawn by hand using flour, rice grains or coloured chalk. They can be circular, square or rectangular, or a combination of multiple shapes.

Create your own rangoli pattern using leaves, flowers, small stones, sand or shells – in fact, whatever you like! You could make a small rangoli pattern out of seeds to feed the birds that live in your garden.

Draw your pattern or take a photo of your finished creation and attach it to the page opposite.

CHALK POWDER

RICE

ENVIRONMENT AND SPACES

MY FAVOURITE PLACE

FEEL!

What is your favourite place outside? Describe it. How does it make you feel?

_____
_____
_____
_____
_____
_____
_____

Share this place with someone. Then ask them to describe their favourite place and how it makes them feel. Can they take you there? Write down what they told you about it here.

_____
_____
_____
_____
_____
_____
_____
_____

MAKE!

CREATE A REAL HABITAT IN MINIATURE

A habitat is a place where an animal naturally lives. Can you re-create a habitat in miniature and make it as realistic as possible?

Here are two ideas. Turn a puddle into a miniature lake. Put tiny pebbles around it to look like boulders, and small twigs with small leaves to look like trees in a forest.

Or, use sand and tiny stones to make a rocky seashore. See if you can find small twigs for driftwood, or tiny pieces of plants to use as seaweed.

Draw a picture of your habitat below or take a photo of it and attach it here. Describe what's in your miniature habitat.

TWIGS

PEBBLES

CREATE AN IMAGINARY HABITAT

Create an imaginary habitat of your own. You can put anything you want in it.

Before you do, think about what it's like. Is it hot or cold? Is it wet or dry? Is it bare or full of life? What plants and animals live there? How are they suited (adapted) to living there? It could even have no gravity, so that everything floats in the air!

Write down some words or a description that gives more information about your habitat.

_____
_____
_____
_____
_____
_____
_____
_____
_____
_____

Now draw a picture of your imaginary habitat on the page opposite.

MYTHICAL BEASTS

This Japanese painting, which was made more than 300 years ago, shows a longma, a phoenix and a dragon. These are all mythological creatures. Can you tell which is which? (Hint: there is information in the fact bubble on the opposite page to help.)

If you have created your own imaginary habitat (see page 44), now is your chance to draw a mythical (made-up, fantastical) beast that lives there.

What features does your beast have? Why does it need these features to live in your habitat? Label these on your picture or write a description underneath your drawing.

FACT
A dragon is a mythological creature that appears in stories from many different cultures around the world. Sometimes it is snake-like in appearance, and sometimes it has wings and breathes fire. A longma is a winged horse with dragon scales from Chinese mythology, and a phoenix is a bird from ancient mythology that dies by bursting into flames, and is then born again from its ashes.

EXPLORING TANIWHA

Taniwha are mystical creatures seen by Māori as part of the natural environment. Taniwha can take the shape of animals and some can move between different forms. Some taniwha are terrifying monsters, while others are kaitiaki, or protectors, of local places and people.

In 1907, a newspaper reported that a taniwha had emerged from the sea at Waimarama in Hawke's Bay. The creature was said to have the head of a dog and a body covered in fur. Below, draw what you think this taniwha looked like, or make a collage of it using pictures of other animals. Why do you think it came ashore?

Taniwha usually live in special places, and often near water such as rivers, lakes and the sea. Are there stories about a taniwha that lives near you? Find out more and then write about it on the page opposite.

Name of taniwha: _____

Where it is found: _____

Story: _____

DESCRIBING NATURE BINGO

Find a spot in nature, and sit and look at your surroundings.

Think of twenty adjectives (describing words) that describe what you can see. For example, 'gloopy' (mud), 'scratchy' (dry grass), 'bumpy' (tree bark), 'velvety' (flowers), 'silvery' (snail's trail).

Write all these words down to use as your bingo words.

_____   _____
_____   _____
_____   _____
_____   _____
_____   _____
_____   _____
_____   _____
_____   _____
_____   _____
_____   _____

Challenge some friends or whānau to play bingo with you in your chosen spot in nature.

Trace enough bingo grids (copied from the example opposite) so that each person playing will have their own bingo grid.

Write an adjective from your list in each of the sixteen squares in every bingo grid. Make sure that each grid has a different selection of words, written in a different order so that no two bingo grids are the same.

Give each person a bingo grid and a pencil.

When you and your friends or whānau are ready, say 'go'. Everyone must explore your spot in nature to try to find the things you saw that inspired your adjectives. As they find something that fits the description, they should cross that word off their grid and write down what they found. For example, if they spot some mud, they could cross out 'gloopy' and write down 'mud'.

When someone in the group has crossed off four words in a row, they shout 'bingo!', and they win.

Keep playing to see who comes second, third, and even fourth.

ORGANISE A TRIP TO A SPECIAL PLACE

Taking a trip to somewhere special is a wonderful way to spend time with friends and whānau. It's even better when it's to somewhere you've always wanted to go.

On the next page, write down where you would like to go and what you need to take with you. The list below will help you get started.

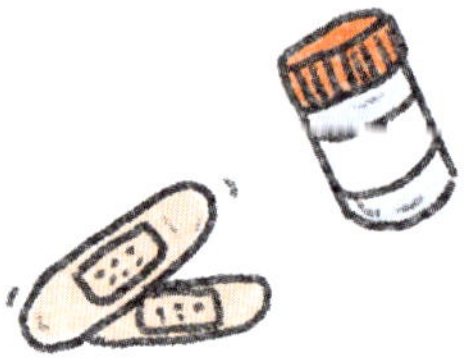

Maps and a means of communication, like a mobile phone

Medication

Emergency equipment

The name and phone number of the person you are telling of your plans in case of emergency

Clothing

Weather protection (including sunblock)

BE PREPARED

If you are heading somewhere outdoors in nature, be prepared. You never know how weather conditions may change. Check out the Department of Conservation's website for a recommended gear list for a day hike (find the link on page 171).

Food and drink

We are going to: _____

We will need:

_____   _____

_____   _____

_____   _____

_____   _____

_____   _____

_____   _____

_____   _____

When you get home, attach some photos of your trip to this page, or write down or draw some of your memories of it.

_____

_____

_____

_____

_____

SOUND SCAVENGER HUNT

Our amazing brains block out lots of background noise for us, so we don't get overwhelmed by the sounds of everything around us. If you listen carefully, you'll be amazed by what you can really hear when you give things your full attention.

How would you describe a sound made far away? How would you describe a sound made close by?

IN A NATURE SPACE, LISTEN FOR:

- ☐ Birdsong
- ☐ The breeze or wind
- ☐ Running water
- ☐ Rustling leaves
- ☐ Crunching rocks or gravel
- ☐ Breaking sticks
- ☐ A splash

What else can you hear?

Make a tick alongside the sounds that you heard and write down any extra sounds you heard.

_____
_____
_____
_____
_____
_____
_____

"CRUNCH"

IN TOWN, LISTEN FOR:

- ☐ Doors closing
- ☐ Cars
- ☐ Motorbikes
- ☐ Horns honking
- ☐ People talking
- ☐ Dogs barking
- ☐ Phones ringing
- ☐ Lawnmowers

What else can you hear?

Make a tick alongside the sounds that you heard and write down any extra sounds you heard.

_____
_____
_____
_____
_____
_____
_____

HONK!

DIGGING HOLES

Using a trowel or spade, dig small holes (make sure you fill them in again when you are finished) in six totally different areas, such as your garden, a beach or the bank of a stream.

Do the holes all look the same inside? Describe each hole below. Is the hole muddy? Is it sandy? Are there stones? What else did you notice?

1. _____
2. _____
3. _____
4. _____
5. _____
6. _____

If you can, glue or tape a bit of the 'ground' on this page as your example.

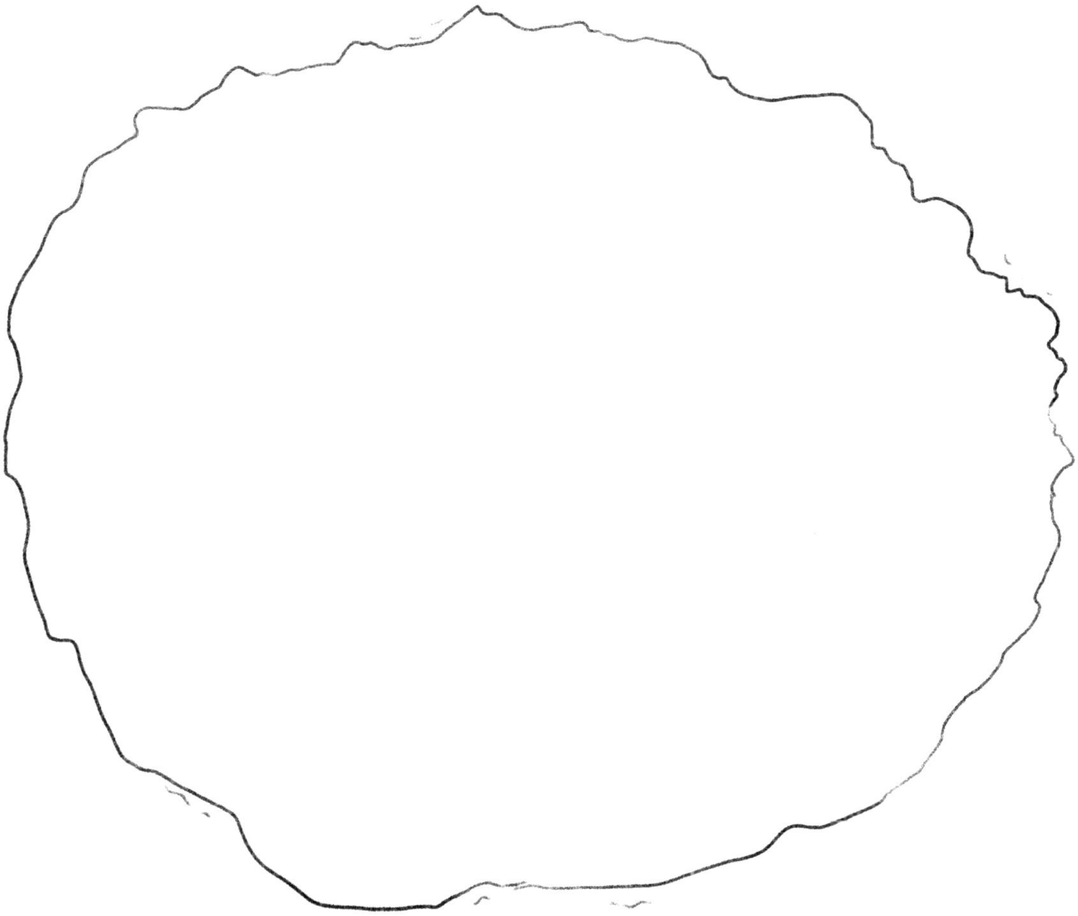

SENSATIONAL SUNCATCHERS

Suncatchers are beautiful and decorative artworks that catch the sunlight filtering through your window. They can be made from really simple materials.

Try collecting things from just one area for your suncatcher, then make another one using things collected from a completely different area. Consider the differences between your suncatchers.

YOU WILL NEED:

Scissors

Paper plate or piece of old cardboard

Crayons or pens

String or nylon

Leaves, flowers, grass, sand, or anything small collected outside that could be attached to the contact paper or tape

Clear contact paper (self-adhesive book covering), or thick, clear tape

WHAT TO DO:

1. Leaving an edge at least 3cm wide all round, cut out the central area of the paper plate, or make a frame from a piece of cardboard.

2. Cut a piece of clear contact paper in the same shape as your frame but about 1–2cm bigger on all sides. Peel off the backing and then stick it to your frame. If you are using tape, stick overlapping strips across the frame.

3. Place your collected leaves, flowers, sand and other items onto the sticky side of the contact paper, inside the frame.

4. Once you've finished, cut another piece of clear contact paper that is 1–2cm bigger than the frame. Peel off the backing and stick it onto the frame so that the sticky sides of both pieces of contact paper are facing one another.

5. Decorate the cardboard frame with crayon or pen.

6. Attach the string or nylon to your suncatcher and hang it in a window so that the light shines through it. Admire your creation!

BIOBLITZ

A bioblitz is a survey of all the living things in an area, usually found within a short period of time.

To carry out your own bioblitz, sit in a spot outside in nature and try to guess (estimate) how many different living things you can see.

What is your guess?

Next, collect evidence of as many different living things that you can find and lay them out on a picnic blanket or old sheet. These may be the leaves of different plants, the shells of different minibeasts, the feathers of different birds and so on – anything you can find that comes from a living thing. If you find a living animal, such as a snail or a worm, for example, record what it is, but leave it where you found it.

What did you find? How many different pieces of evidence did you find? Was your guess (estimate) of the number of living things close to the actual number you found? What does the evidence you found tell you about what lives in the area? Write this all down here.

BIOBLITZ COLLAGE

Using tape or glue, stick items from your bioblitz to this page to show the habitat you surveyed. Make sure you don't attach anything that is still alive!

THEN, NOW AND... LATER?

Find a spot outside (anywhere will do) and try to imagine what it might have looked like 100 years ago.

What things can you see that would not have existed 100 years ago?

_____
_____
_____
_____

What things might have been around 100 years ago that we can't see now?

_____
_____
_____
_____

What things do you think are the same?

_____
_____
_____
_____

What might be around 100 years in the future?

_____
_____
_____
_____

WONDERFUL WOOD

People make lots of things out of 'natural resources' – materials and things that come from nature. Wood is one example of a natural resource. We use wood from many different kinds of trees to make all sorts of objects.

Write down as many things you can think of that are made out of wood. If you need inspiration, walk around your house or school and see what you can spot.

PEOPLE AND ENVIRONMENTS

Look at this picture. How have people changed this environment?

You can see that trees have been cut down, possibly to make some of the things you identified in the '*Wonderful wood*' activity (see page 61). But we don't cut trees down just to make products from them. Once the trees have been cut down, what else could people do with the space that has been cleared?

What else can you see in the picture?

NATURAL RESOURCES

Look at a space – either inside or outside. How many natural resources can you see that we use in our everyday lives?

Look for and write down as many of these that you can think of.

- Plants or animals we eat, such as spinach or chicken

_____
_____
_____

- Plants that produce things we use, such as trees for wood

_____
_____
_____

- Animals that produce things we eat, such as hens for eggs and cows for milk

_____
_____
_____

- Animals that produce things we use, such as sheep for wool and cows for leather

_____
_____

If you're not sure how these things are produced, do some research and see what you can find.

ATUA IN TE AO MĀORI

In te ao Māori, or the Māori world, there are many atua, or ancestral gods, goddesses and guardians of environments and environmental conditions.

Think about the time of day, temperature and conditions you are in. What atua might be present?

Can you find something that represents any of the atua on these pages? For example, could you draw or take a photo of the moon to represent Hine? Or could you paint a picture of a sunrise to represent Hine-tītama? Or perhaps a photo of waves crashing onto rocks represents Hinemoana to you. Draw inside each of the boxes or attach your photos.

PAPATŪĀNUKU
Earth mother

HINE
The female personification of the moon

HINE-ATA-UIRA OR HINE-TĪTAMA
The goddess of dawn

HINEMOANA
A goddess of the ocean

HINE-PARAWHENUAMEA
Guardian of fresh water

HINE-PŪ-KOHU-RANGI
The goddess of the mist

HINEWAI
The female personification of light misty rain

ALIVE, ALIVE ONCE OR NEVER ALIVE?

Environments are made up of many different things, some of which are alive and some of which are not. The things that are not alive may have been alive once (like a dead leaf, which was once a living part of a plant), but other things have never been alive (like a rock).

Look around you and find things that fall into all three groups – alive, alive once and never alive. List five of them in each of the three columns below.

ALIVE	ALIVE ONCE	NEVER ALIVE

If you find anything you're not sure about, how could you find out what group it fits in? Who could you ask?

LOOKING AT LAYERS

Look at the photograph below. What do you notice, or observe? Can you see layers in the cliff that look a bit like stripes? What do you think they are?

_____

_____

_____

_____

Can you find a bank or a cliff face in your local area that also has this kind of layering? It might be difficult or even impossible to look closely at each layer safely, but if you can, explore how the layers are different. These layers built up through a process called sedimentation. You can find out more about this below.

Draw a picture of what you have found or take a photo and attach it here. What can you find out about it? Think about the following questions:

- Why are there layers?
- What might the different layers be made of?
- How were these different layers formed?

FACT
Sedimentation is the action or process of laying down, or depositing, little bits of rocks, minerals, sand, fossils and other matter (sediments). This might be from water, ice or wind. Over time, new layers (strata) pile up and press down, eventually forcing excess water out of the layers, and a solid mass forms.

EXPERIMENTS AND ENQUIRY

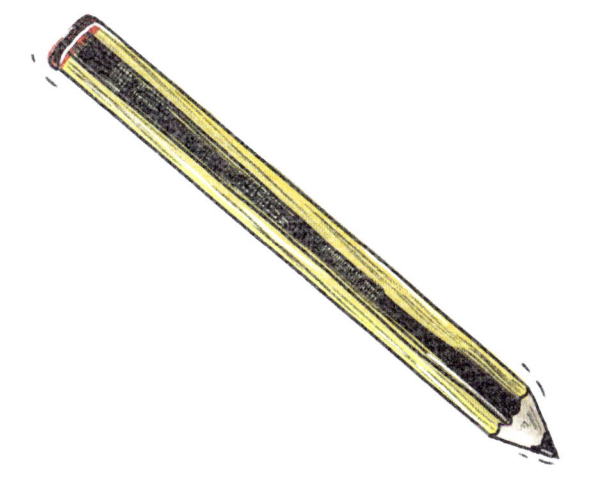

CURIOSITY IS KING

Watch something happening that you find interesting. It might be the rain falling, a bird eating, popcorn popping, your dog drinking water, a spider making a web or your brother putting on a coat to go outside. Write it here.

I am watching: _____

Come up with ten different questions about the activity (don't worry if you think finding the answer might be impossible). Think about the question words, like 'what', 'how', 'why', 'when', 'will', 'do' and 'where' if you get stuck. Write your questions down here.

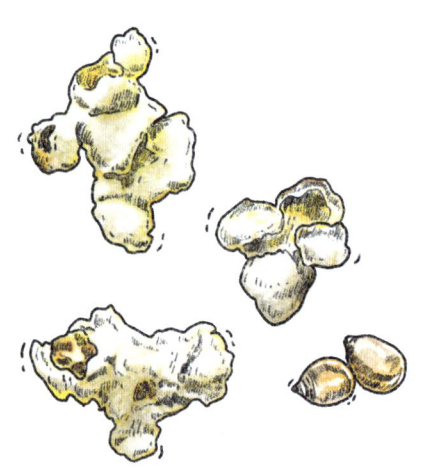

IDEAS

Why are there different kinds of rain? Why do birds eat worms? Will popcorn pop without oil in the pot? Do dogs only like to drink water? Do spiders make webs of different shapes?

1. _____
2. _____
3. _____
4. _____
5. _____
6. _____
7. _____
8. _____
9. _____
10. _____

Choose your favourite question or the thing you really want to know. Write it here.

_____
_____

What are the different 'parts' of what you are seeing and who or what is involved?

_____
_____
_____
_____

What might you need in order to find an answer to your questions? Do you need any equipment or tools? Do you need to investigate it at a particular time?

_____
_____
_____
_____

What 'thing' (called a variable) would you watch or change to see if it had an effect on the activity? For example, to find out if the weather affects the food birds eat, you need to watch the weather. To decide if the type of material on which a spider builds its web affects the shape of the web, you need to look at different materials with spider webs on them.

_____
_____
_____
_____

A CHALLENGE

What's a cool experiment you would like to challenge others to complete?

_____
_____

What will they need to complete your challenge?

_____
_____
_____
_____

What are the steps they need to take?

_____
_____
_____
_____
_____
_____

Did you challenge someone to carry out your experiment? Ask them for their results and write them down here.

_____
_____
_____
_____
_____

What did you find out?

_____
_____
_____

THE SAME, BUT DIFFERENT

Find ten of the same things from nature, such as ten leaves, ten flowers or ten ants.

Look at your objects closely. Are they all *exactly* the same? How are they different? It may help to use a magnifying glass or hand lens if your objects are small.

Photograph or draw your objects in the space above to show their differences.

What does this tell you about all the living things in nature? We may think that individuals of the same kind of plant or animal are the same, but are they?

NATURE'S DYES

MAKE!

People make fabric and clothes in all different colours, but how do they do that? What materials from nature can be used to dye things different colours?

The experiment on the opposite page makes dyes from plant materials. Before you start, make a guess (prediction) of the colour you think each plant will dye your cloth.

RED CABBAGE

BEETROOT

SPINACH

STRAWBERRIES

TEA BAGS

ROSES

CARROTS

MINT

TURMERIC

BAY LEAVES

TIP
Once you've finished this experiment, you may like to make a larger batch of your favourite dye to colour a T-shirt or other item of clothing for you to wear. You could reuse an old piece of white or light-coloured clothing, or buy something suitable from an op shop.

'NATURE'S DYES'

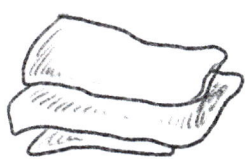

YOU WILL NEED:

Scissors (make sure to ask an adult if you need help)

Clean old white cloth or T-shirt

Plant materials for making dyes, such as red cabbage, spinach or mint leaves, bay leaves, turmeric, celery leaves, carrots, onion skins, blackberries, red and pink roses, avocado skins, beetroot, walnut shells, tea leaves, coffee grinds

Chopping board and sharp knife

Glasses, jars or small containers (as many as the colours you want to try)

Warm or hot water to make dyes (but cool water will also work)

Cold water for rinsing (a nearby tap will do)

Optional – glue, tape or a stapler to attach your colour samples to your book

WHAT TO DO:

1. Using scissors, cut the cloth or T-shirt into small squares measuring approximately 3cm by 3cm.

2. Roughly chop the plant material. (Ask an adult to help if you need it.)

3. Line up your glasses, jars or small containers and add a small amount of warm or hot water (at least 50ml) to each.

4. Add some of the plant materials to each glass, making sure you use only one material per glass so that you can test its colour. For best results, 'brew' the material in the water for at least an hour and leave it to cool before using it as a dye.

5. Place a square of fabric in each glass of dye and leave it for at least an hour to soak in the colour. If you want a deeper colour, what could you do?

6. Rinse the square in cold water and hang it out to dry.

7. Check out your result. Was your prediction right?

If you want to display your results, attach your dyed squares to this page.

Keep your dyes for the 'Colour mixing', 'Can you change the colour of a flower?' and 'Make your own paper' activities on pages 76, 77 and 162.

Colour MIXING

MAKE!

Can you make a range of colours by mixing different individual dyes together?

YOU WILL NEED:

Your dyes from the 'Nature's dyes' activity on page 74

Some more glasses, jars or small containers for mixing

WHAT TO DO:

1. Mix your natural dyes together in different amounts to make different colours. How could you make purple? Try it!

2. Drip some of the dyes onto this page to create splodges of colour. Keep a note of what you used to create each colour so that you can make it again next time.

TIP

Keep these new colours for the 'Can you change the colour of a flower?' experiment on the opposite page.

SNAP!

CAN YOU CHANGE THE COLOUR OF A FLOWER?

Is this possible? It sounds like magic!

YOU WILL NEED:

Food colouring (try red, blue or yellow to start), or your dyes from pages 75 or 76

White flowers such as daisies, carnations or lilies - pick them just before your experiment

Vase, glass or tall container

WHAT TO DO:

1. Place three tablespoons of coloured dye in the vase or glass.
2. Cut the flower stem and immediately place it in the vase.
3. Watch the flower on and off over the next hour. What happens?

___
___

4. Take a photo or draw a picture of the result and attach it to this page.

FACT
Inside the stems of plants are tiny tubes called xylem. Water travels up these xylem into the stems, leaves and flowers of the plant. In this experiment, the xylem pull the coloured water up into the flowers.

Can you explain what has happened? Think about the dye. Where did it go?

___
___
___

77

WHY DO TREE LEAVES CHANGE COLOUR?

In autumn, you may have noticed that the leaves on some trees change colour.

Can you remember what colours the leaves were before they changed?

_____

_____

What colours did they change to?

_____

_____

What happens to the leaves after they change colour? What texture do they have – are they soft or crunchy?

_____

_____

When do some leaves change colour?

_____

_____

Why do you think some leaves change colour?

_____

_____

Come to think of it, why are trees green? (What's *in* the leaf?)

_____

_____

_____

_____

WHAT'S HAPPENING?

Leaves are green because they have a green pigment, like a dye, called chlorophyll. As autumn approaches, the plant stops putting this green pigment into the leaves. With the green colour gone, other red, orange and yellow pigments (that were there all along) show more clearly on the fallen leaves.

SINK OR FLOAT?

Think about this: Why do some things float and some things sink? Can you guess if something will float or sink just by looking at it?

YOU WILL NEED:

Large bowl filled with water

Selection of fruits and vegetables – for example, capsicum, strawberry, nectarine, carrot, apple, blueberry, courgette, potato, rock melon

WHAT TO DO:

1. Feel each fruit and vegetable and describe it. Is it heavy or light? Is it very dense (heavy for its size) or not so dense? What shape is it?
2. Guess (predict) whether the object will sink or float.
3. Place each fruit and vegetable in the water in turn. Record what happens for each one.

Can you see any patterns in your results? Do the weight, density or shape make a difference to whether something sinks or floats?

What happens if you cut into each fruit or vegetable? Do they still sink or float? What do you notice? (You might want to make a fruit or vegetable salad now, so there's no waste!)

SINK OR FLOAT?

CAPSICUM?   WATERMELON?   BLUEBERRIES?

DOWN THE DRAIN?

How many sinks or drains do you have at home? Can you think of all the things you and your family put down them? It's not just water ...

Over a week, try to record *everything* you see your family putting down the drain. Record them here.

IN THE KITCHEN	IN THE BATHROOM	IN THE LAUNDRY

THE DRAINS OUTSIDE

Do you put any chemicals like fertiliser on your garden or pot plants? Do these things also end up down the drain? Think about when you get heavy rain. What really washes down the drains?

All the different products we put down our drains mix with water and end up being called 'grey water'. Where do you think all this grey water might end up?

_____
_____
_____

Do you think there are better choices for the kinds of products we use at home every day?

_____
_____
_____

Are there more natural products we could use instead of chemicals? Can you name some of these?

_____
_____
_____
_____
_____
_____

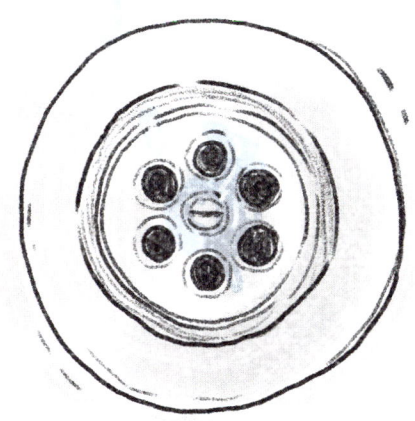

POLLUTED CELERY

Plants need fresh water to survive. Fresh water does not just exist in streams, rivers and lakes – it can also be found in soil and underground.

What happens if we pollute this fresh water by pouring things on the ground, or down the drain at home, at work or at school?

This easy experiment with celery shows how pollution in the water affects plants. See 'Can you change the colour of a flower?' on page 77 to find out how this happens.

HINT
Read about this 'grey water' in the 'Down the drain' activity on page 80.

YOU WILL NEED:

Blue or red food colouring

Vase or glass of water (about one-third full)

Bunch of celery

Chopping board

Knife (and maybe the help of an adult)

WHAT TO DO:

1. Add four drops of your chosen food colouring to the water in your vase or glass.
2. Cut two sticks of celery off the bunch at the very bottom and place them in the glass or vase. Choose stems from the middle of the bunch, not from the outside. Guess (predict) what will happen.
3. Leave the stems for three hours.
4. After three hours, choose one of the stems and cut it into pieces across the length of the stem. (Ask an adult to help you if you need it). Look inside the cut pieces. What do you notice? Write a description of what you see.

_____

_____

_____

5. Leave the other celery stick in the glass or vase for a full day (twenty-four hours), then cut it into pieces in the same way. What do you notice? Write a description of what you see.

_____

_____

_____

Think about all the plants living around us, in our gardens, parks and forests. What would happen to them if more and more pollution was added to the water that ends up in the soil, streams and other waterways? What would that mean for the plants we eat? Where would that pollution eventually end up?

_____

_____

_____

_____

_____

HOW IS WATER USED IN YOUR HOUSE?

Walk around your house, inside and outside, and find every single point where you can use or access water. Note your findings here.

_____
_____
_____
_____
_____

What are some of the ways you use water in and around your home?

_____
_____
_____
_____
_____

What do you think is 'responsible' (good) water use and 'irresponsible' (not so good) water use? Think about what happens when you leave the tap on versus turning it off while you brush your teeth, or having a ten-minute shower versus a three-minute shower.

_____
_____
_____
_____
_____

Are any of the ways you use water examples of irresponsible water use, and why?

_____
_____
_____
_____
_____

What are some other examples of irresponsible water use?

_____
_____
_____
_____
_____

What could you do to stop any irresponsible use of water in your house?

_____
_____
_____
_____
_____

WHAT DOES YOUR HOUSE PUT INTO LANDFILL?

Landfill is another name for all the rubbish at your house that can't be recycled and ends up in a rubbish dump or tip. That means anything you put in the bin. Cling film, food scraps that aren't composted and some plastics all go into landfill. But how much does each house add?

Can you guess how much rubbish in your house goes into landfill over a month? What units would you use to measure this? The number of rubbish bins? Weight in kilograms?

My guess is:

_____
_____
_____

What could you do to really find out how much waste your house produces in a month?

_____
_____
_____
_____

What information would you write down, or record?

_____
_____
_____
_____
_____
_____
_____

How long would you collect this information for?

___

Did you do it? What did you find out?

___

___

___

What is your conclusion (decision)?

___

___

___

Challenge a friend to do the same thing. Whose house put more rubbish into the landfill in a month?

___

Are there differences between your two houses that might mean one would produce more rubbish than the other? List all these differences here. (For example, do the same number of people live in both houses?)

___

___

___

___

___

___

___

___

___

TRACKING THE SUN

Make this cool sundial to track the sun and tell the time.

YOU WILL NEED:

Two sunny, cloudless days

Marker pen

Paper plate

Sharp pencil

Ruler

Compass

Metal straw

Thumbtacks or nails

WHAT TO DO:

1. On a sunny day, use a marker pen to write the number '12' at the very edge of the paper plate. This number is going to represent 12 o'clock noon.

2. Take your sharp pencil and push it through the very middle of the paper plate. You will be left with a hole.

3. Use the ruler to draw a straight line from the '12' to the hole in the middle of the plate.

4. Head outside with a compass and your plate shortly before noon. You now need to find your closest 'celestial pole' (this pole is parallel with the Earth's axis, which is the invisible line through the centre of the Earth that the planet spins around). If you live in the southern hemisphere, find south on your compass (or find north if you live in the northern hemisphere).

5. Place the plate on the ground where it will get full sun all day. Stick the straw through the hole in the middle of the plate and push it slightly forward so that it leans in the direction of your closest celestial pole (that's south in Aotearoa New Zealand).

6. At exactly noon, rotate the plate so that the straw's shadow lies along the line you drew from the number '12' to the middle of the plate. Since you are only measuring the hours of daylight with your sundial, the plate will end up showing twelve points (like a clock).

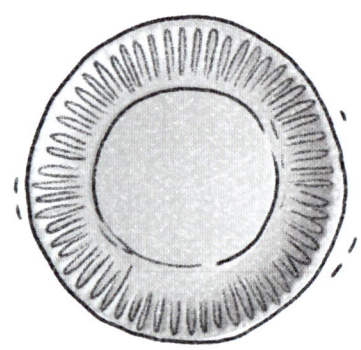
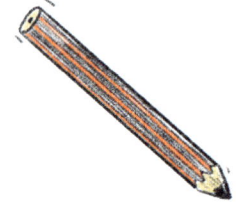

7. Poke a few thumbtacks or nails through the plate into the ground so that it stays fixed in place. Set an alarm for 1pm or set a timer for an hour's time.

8. At 1pm go back to the plate and check the position of the straw's shadow. Write the number '1' at the very edge of the plate, exactly where you see the shadow falling.

9. Go back outside on exactly every hour, at 2pm, 3pm, 4pm and so on until the sun goes down. Continue marking the position of the straw's shadow on the edge of the plate and writing down the number of the hour.

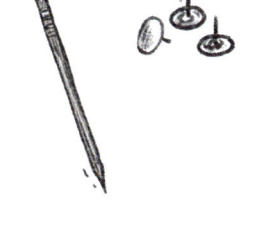

10. Resume marking the hours on your plate the next morning through until 11am, then double check at noon that the shadow from the straw lies along the line you drew to the number '12'.

Your sundial is complete! On the next sunny day, use your sundial to tell the time by checking which number the shadow points to. Why do you think the shadow moves around the points on your plate? Did you notice that the shadow moves in a clockwise direction?

Draw a picture of your sundial or take a photo of it and attach it here.

draw here!

WHY DO BIRDS HAVE DIFFERENT-SHAPED BEAKS?

Look at the birds opposite. What do you notice about their beaks? Are they all the same? How are they different?

_____
_____
_____
_____

Why do you think birds have different-shaped beaks? (Think about what each bird feeds on and how it eats.)

_____
_____
_____
_____

Where could you find out more information?

_____
_____

What did you find out?

_____
_____
_____
_____
_____

MAKE!

WHAT ATTRACTS DIFFERENT BIRDS?

As we observed in the activity 'Why do birds have different-shaped beaks?' (see page 90), different birds eat different things.

Here are three different bird feeders you can make and put in your garden or another outside space to attract birds. Look at the design and the food in each of these bird feeders. Guess (predict) and write down which birds they might attract.

Guess:
1. _____
2. _____
3. _____

TIP
For more ideas for bird feeders, see the 'Homemade bird treats' activity on page 158.

Record the types of birds that come to your feeders. Were your guesses (predictions) correct?

Record:
1. _____
2. _____
3. _____

1. Cut a hole at least the size of a golf ball about halfway down the side of a screw-top plastic jar. Cover the bottom of the jar with mealworms. Screw the jar to a fence or similar structure. To add more mealworms, remove the lid of the jar.

2. Cut an orange or apple in half and spear it on a stick. Push the other end of the stick into the ground or a pot plant.

3. Put cut red grapes in a clear, shallow dish. Place the dish on an outside table or in the fork or branches of a tree.

DESIGN A TŪĪ FEEDER

Can you design a bird feeder for a tūī? It could be one you hang in your garden or outside a window.

To help with your design, think about the tūī's beak shape and what it eats. What kind of food do you need to put in the feeder? How does a tūī need to access the food to eat it?

Write down the materials you need to make your tūī feeder.

_____
_____
_____
_____
_____

Once you've made your feeder, put it outside. Did it attract any tūī? Was your feeder successful?

_____
_____
_____
_____

Take a photo of your feeder and attach it here or draw a picture of it.

COLLECT!

FINDING EVIDENCE OF LIFE

How do you know that there are living things around you, even if you can't see them? What signs, or 'evidence', can you find to give you some ideas?

Try to find each of the items below and write down what they might be evidence of.

_____
_____
_____
_____

FEATHER

BURROW

FOOTPRINT

NEST

SLIME TRAIL

WHAT IS A ROCK?

What is a rock? Do some research if you need to. What did you find out?

_____
_____
_____

Is a rock a living thing or a non-living thing? Why do you think that?

_____
_____

Write down all the different words for 'rock' you can think of – for example, pebble, gravel and so on.

_____
_____
_____

What kind of rock is pounamu?

_____
_____
_____

Why is this rock important to Māori?

_____
_____
_____
_____

WHY ARE ROCKS DIFFERENT SHAPES?

Look at these different types of rock. What shapes do you see and why do you think these rocks might be different shapes? For example, what do you think has happened to some rocks to make their edges smooth? Or why might a rock have jagged, sharp edges? Write your answers under each picture.

WHAT IS A MINERAL?

What is a mineral? Try to describe it in your own words. Do some research if you need to. What did you find out?

What is the difference between a rock and a mineral? (Hint: look back at the 'What is a rock?' activity on page 95).

Minerals can be described by a number of different features. Some of these are listed below. Can you match each feature to its correct definition (answers below)?

FEATURE	DEFINITION
1. Colour	A. How heavy the mineral feels
2. Lustre	B. What the mineral's surface looks like in the light (dull or shiny)
3. Specific gravity	C. The pattern formed when the mineral is broken
4. Crystal form	D. The mineral's ability (or not) to let light pass through
5. Cleavage	E. A measure of the mineral's toughness – how easily (or not) it falls apart
6. Tenacity	F. What the mineral can scratch and what can scratch the mineral
7. Hardness	G. The apparent colour of the mineral
8. Transparency	H. The shape of the mineral when it is a crystal

Can you find five examples of minerals?

Answers: 1 = G, 2 = B, 3 = A, 4 = H, 5 = C, 6 = E, 7 = F, 8 = D

SOLID AS A ROCK ... OR NOT?

Rocks are a bit like cakes, in that they are made out of two or more ingredients, but rocks are made out of minerals.

As you saw in the 'What is a mineral?' activity (see page 97), 'hardness' is one of the features that can be used to identify a mineral. Different minerals have different measures of hardness, or, in other words, some minerals are 'harder' or 'softer' than others.

Mineral hardness is measured on the Mohs scale, which is based on how easily one mineral can scratch another. Rock with a measure of 1 is the softest (like talc), while 10 is very, very hard (like a diamond).

You can find out the hardness of the minerals in a rock by scratching the rock with a range of different materials. If the item you use to scratch the rock is harder than the minerals in the rock, then it will mark the rock with a scratch. But if the rock is harder than the item you use, the rock will not be marked.

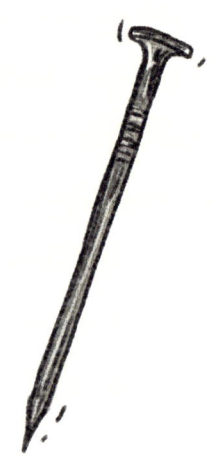

YOU WILL NEED:

Safety goggles or glasses

Protective clothing

Selection of different rocks – pumice, limestone, river stones, pebbles off the beach

Your fingernail (Mohs hardness 2.5)

Coin – try to find a foreign copper coin (Mohs hardness 3)

Piece of glass – try to find one with smooth edges, like sea glass (Mohs hardness 5.5–6.5)

Steel nail (Mohs hardness 6.5–7.5)

Piece of quartz (Mohs hardness 7)

WHAT TO DO:

1. Put on your safety goggles and protective clothing and cover the surface you're working on with newspaper.

2. Starting with the first rock, test how hard it is by trying to scratch it. Use your fingernail first, then the copper coin, the glass, the nail and finally the quartz. If you think you have made a scratch, rub it with your thumb. If it's just powder, it will rub off – that doesn't count as a scratch. If it really is a scratch, it will still be there, even after you rub it.

3. In the table opposite, tick the column of the first item that made a scratch in the rock. For example, if you finally scratched a rock with the steel nail (but not the fingernail, coin or glass), then tick the 'Steel nail' column only.

4. In the 'Hardness' column, record the Mohs hardness measure of your rock. To work this out, look at the Mohs hardness values in the list of materials on the left, and the ticks in your table. An item will leave a scratch if it is the same hardness as, or harder than, the rock sample.

If you make a scratch on the rock, the hardness of the minerals in the rock is probably somewhere between the hardness of the item you used to scratch it and the softer item you tried before it. For example, if the glass scratches the rock but the copper coin doesn't, then the hardness of the rock minerals is somewhere between that of the copper (Mohs hardness 3) and the glass (Mohs hardness 5.5–6.5) – in other words, the Mohs hardness of the rock will be between 3–5.5. Write down this number in the 'Hardness' column.

5. Repeat for all of your rock samples.

What is the order of hardness from your rock samples? Which rock has the greatest hardness? Which one has the lowest hardness?

How could you find out what minerals your rocks are made from? For example, where could you research to find out what a coin is made out of?

IMPORTANT: THINK ABOUT HEALTH AND SAFETY!

Work with an adult.
Wear safety goggles or glasses.
Wear protective clothing – some powder may be produced as you scratch the rocks.
Try not to inhale any of the dust.
Cover the surface you're working on with a sheet of old newspaper.
Be careful not to scratch yourself with the steel nail.

ROCK TYPE	FINGERNAIL	COIN	GLASS	STEEL NAIL	QUARTZ	HARDNESS

SENSE AND MINDFULNESS

PEACE OF MIND

What activity makes you feel calm or gives you peace of mind?

_____
_____
_____
_____

Where do you do this activity? Do you need anything for it?

_____
_____
_____
_____

Encourage your friends or whānau to try the activity. How do they feel when they do it?

_____
_____
_____
_____
_____
_____
_____
_____
_____
_____

SENSING NATURE

Find a spot and get comfortable. Now, try to name:

TEN THINGS YOU CAN SEE

_____
_____
_____
_____
_____
_____
_____
_____
_____
_____

SIX THINGS YOU CAN TOUCH

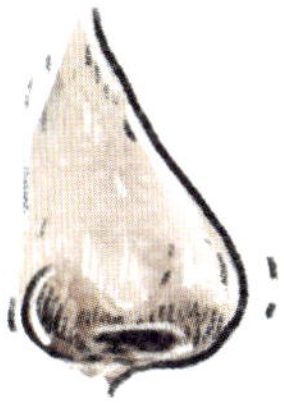

_____
_____
_____
_____
_____
_____

TWO THINGS YOU CAN SMELL

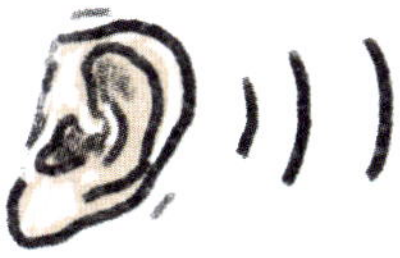

_____
_____

FOUR THINGS YOU CAN HEAR

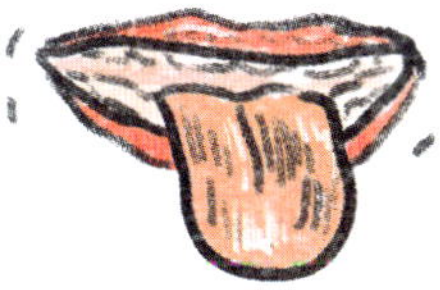

_____
_____
_____
_____

ONE THING YOU CAN TASTE

_____

COUNTLESS KAPUA

Find a comfortable spot outside on a day when there are kapua, or clouds, in the sky. Now just lie down and watch them! What shapes can you see?

'Meteorology' is the study of the atmosphere to learn about weather. In meteorology, there are four main types of cloud: cirrus, stratus, cumulus and nimbus (all pictured opposite).

Some of the Māori names for kapua are: pīpipi (cirrostratus clouds), pūtahi (long stratus clouds), pūrehurehu (cirrus clouds), taipua (cumulus clouds bunching together in rounded masses), okewa (nimbus clouds).

What kind of clouds are you looking at? Do you think a particular type of cloud form is the best for cloud watching?

___

___

___

___

Over time, can you spot all the kapua types pictured? Write the dates you saw them below.

DATE OBSERVED	TYPE

DID YOU KNOW?
Nephelococcygia (say 'neph-e-lo-kok-ku-gi-a') is the word for seeking and finding shapes in clouds.

PŪREHUREHU / 'CIRRUS'

High, wispy clouds (their name comes from the Latin word for 'curl of hair')

TAIPUA / CUMULUS

Fluffy clouds (their name comes from the Latin word for 'heap' or 'pile')

PŪTAHI / STRATUS

Featureless, layered clouds (their name comes from the Italian word for 'layer')

OKEWA / NIMBUS

Multi-level grey clouds that produce rain or snow (their name comes from the Latin word for 'rain')

THE TAMARIKI OF TĀWHIRIMĀTEA

In Māori tradition, the god Tāwhirimātea – one of the children of the sky father Ranginui and the Earth mother Papatūānuku – controls the weather. Tāwhirimātea had a number of tamariki, or children, including a variety of clouds. Can you spot his tamariki in the sky?

Write down the date that you saw them, where, and at what time.

AOKANAPANAPA
Clouds reflecting glowing red light

Where:

Date:

Time:

AONUI
Dense clouds

Where:

Date:

Time:

AOPAKAREA
Clouds of thunderstorms

Where:

Date:

Time:

AOTAKAWE
Clouds hurriedly flying

Where:

Date:

Time:

AOPŌURI
Dark clouds

Where:

Date:

Time:

AOWHĒTUMA
Fiery clouds

Where:

Date:

Time:

MAKE!

WIND CHIMES

What music can you make with Tāwhirimātea's wind tamariki? Collect objects from nature to create beautiful wind chimes.

YOU WILL NEED:

String, twine, nylon or another material to tie your chimes onto the stick

Ruler

Scissors

At least one big stick to hang your chimes off

Objects from nature to act as chimes. Choose things you like the sound of when they knock together (try shells, pieces of driftwood and pine cones)

WHAT TO DO:

1. Cut different lengths of string or other material about 25–40cm long.

2. Tie all the pieces of string to the stick so that they are evenly spaced along its length.

3. Tie one of your chimes to the loose end of one of the pieces of string, then repeat this for all the other strings.

4. Hold your wind chimes up to make sure you are happy with the arrangement. You can vary the length of the string to your liking, but make sure that some of the chimes are at the same height so that they knock against one another, otherwise they won't make a noise.

5. Cut one length of string about 60cm long, and tie to each end of the stick. Hang your wind chime outside in a breezy spot.

TIP
You could recycle materials like ribbons used to wrap up presents as your 'string'.

FINDING TĀWHIRIMĀTEA'S WIND TAMARIKI

Which of Tāwhirimātea's wind tamariki, or children, is blowing today? One from the north (tūāraki), one from the south (tonga), one from the east (marangai) or one from the west (hauāuru)? The direction each child was sent to became the name of that wind.

Weathervanes can help us find this out. Follow the instructions below to make a weathervane.

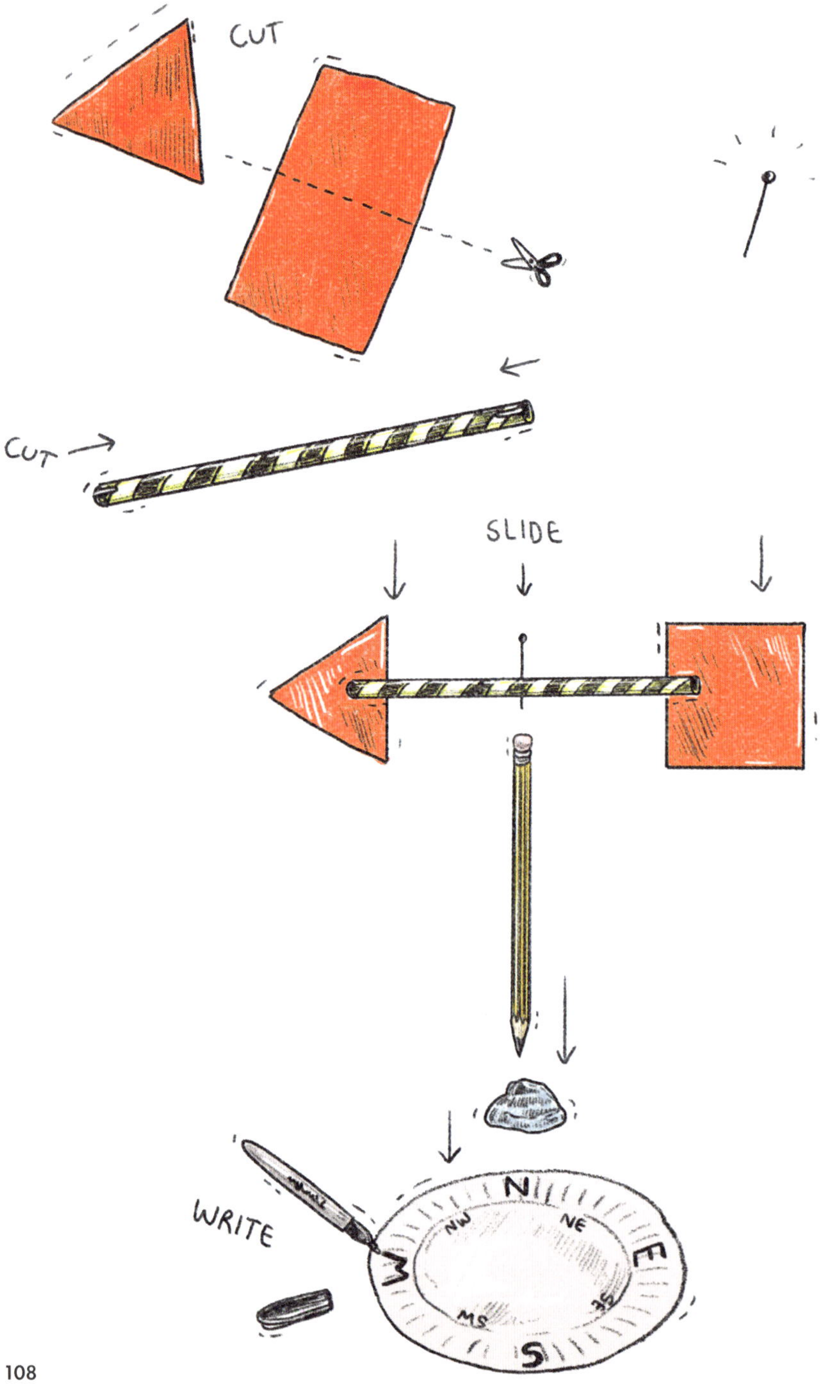

CUT

CUT →

SLIDE

YOU WILL NEED:
Thin cardboard (any colour)
Pencil with an eraser on the end
Ruler
Scissors
Paper straw
Glue or tape (if needed)
Sewing pin
Modelling clay or Blu-Tack®
Paper plate
Marker pens
Compass

WRITE

WHAT TO DO:

1. Using your pencil, draw a triangle measuring about 8cm along each edge on your cardboard and cut it out. This triangle will be the arrow point of your weathervane.

2. Draw an 8cm by 8cm square on your cardboard and cut it out. This square will be the other end of your arrow.

3. Cut a 1cm lengthwise slit on each side of the paper drinking straw at one end. Now do the same at the other end of the straw.

4. Slide your triangle arrow point into the slits at one end of the straw so that the point is facing out, then slide the square into the slits at the other end to make the arrow. If you have trouble keeping the triangle and square in place, use tape or glue to secure them to the straw.

5. Find the middle of the straw and push the pin through this point, from the top through to the bottom.

6. Holding the pencil upright with the eraser at the top, take your arrow and push the bottom of the pin into the middle of the eraser (ask an adult to help you if you have trouble). Leave a little gap between the straw and the eraser. When you view it from the side, the arrow sitting on top of the pencil should now look like a big 'T' shape. When you blow onto the triangle or the square, the arrow should spin freely around the pin on top of your pencil. If it doesn't, make the gap between the straw and the eraser wider.

7. Roll a piece of modelling clay or Blu-Tack® into a ball. Press the point of your pencil deeply into the clay. If your pencil keeps falling over, make the ball bigger so that it is heavier and can support more weight.

8. Get your paper plate and markers. Write 'Tu/N' (for tūāraki/north) at the top of the plate. Then, go clockwise and write 'M/E' (for marangai/east) on the right side, 'To/S' (for tonga/south) on the bottom and 'H/W' (for hauāuru/west) on the left side.

9. Take your weathervane and press the clay ball into the very centre of the plate to keep it in place. The pencil should now be fixed in place upright on the plate and the straw should still spin freely around the pin if you blow on the triangle or square.

10. Take your weathervane outside and put it on a flat table or stool. Don't place it behind any objects that can block the wind – putting it out in the open is better.

11. Use your compass to find the direction of north, then turn the weathervane until the 'N' faces in this direction.

12. Wait for your weathervane to start spinning in the wind. The arrow will point in the direction the wind is coming from.

Which of Tāwhirimātea's wind tamariki is blowing today?

_____

IT'S THE LITTLE THINGS

Choose some objects and look at them closely through a hand lens or magnifying glass. What can you see that you couldn't see with just your eyes? Think about some words you can use to describe what you *see*. Think of all the things you can describe about what you see, like colour, shape and pattern.

Now think about words you can use to describe what you *feel* when you touch the object. This could be its texture or even its temperature. Is it rough or smooth? Is it warm or cold?

Write down your descriptions here.

OBJECT ONE
Name:

See:

Feel:

OBJECT TWO
Name:

See:

Feel:

OBJECT THREE
Name:

See:

Feel:

OBJECT FOUR
Name:

See:

Feel:

SEED

MARBLE

Now, read out your great describing words (adjectives) to a friend without showing them the objects. Can they guess what each of the objects is just from your descriptions?

GET DOWN TO EARTH

What is the ground beneath your feet?

In five different locations, find, feel and describe the 'ground' where you are standing. You could feel the ground with your hands, but consider using your feet too.

What does the ground feel like to touch? What adjectives (describing words) could you use to explain what you feel?

LOCATION	FEEL	DESCRIBE

Find out what you can about the Earth mother, Papatūānuku. Why is she so important?

TIP
Link this activity to the 'Digging holes' one on page 56.

COLLECT!

WHAT'S IN THE BAG?

We rely on our sense of sight to give us lots of information about the world around us. But when we can't use our sight, our other senses can become sharper. Play this guessing game with a friend to find out how many objects they can guess without seeing them.

TIP
You can use the bag you make in the 'T-shirt bags' activity on page 136 as your mystery bag.

BEWARE
Do not to choose sharp or spiky objects that could cause injury to the person you are challenging. If there is any risk with any object you put in the bag, make sure you warn the person before they stick their hand inside!

YOU WILL NEED:

Objects from nature – try different shells, whole fruit or vegetables, stones and nuts

Cloth bag – see 'Tip' (you shouldn't be able to see through the bag)

WHAT TO DO:

1. Hide each object, one at a time, in the cloth bag.

2. Ask your friend to figure out what the object is. They can put their hand in the bag to feel the object, or shake it or smell it, but they mustn't peek!

3. Make the game harder by using objects that have very similar shapes. Think about using a lime and a lemon. Why would this be a challenge?

SENSORY BOX

Collect twelve objects from nature that have different textures, including those you love the feel of, and put them into a box. List the objects here:

1. _____   7. _____
2. _____   8. _____
3. _____   9. _____
4. _____   10. _____
5. _____   11. _____
6. _____   12. _____

Try to think of a really good adjective (describing word) for how each object feels, or even how it makes you feel. Write them down here.

1. _____   7. _____
2. _____   8. _____
3. _____   9. _____
4. _____   10. _____
5. _____   11. _____
6. _____   12. _____

> **TIP**
> It's great to share sensory boxes with very young children (aged one to three years). At this age, they are learning a lot about their world, including recognising things that are the same and those that are different. They are also learning how to make small movements with their hands and fingers, like pinching, and are using language more. But they also like to put things in their mouths, so make sure the sensory box doesn't contain anything too small or dangerous for them.

You could create collections of objects, such as a geology box, a 'smooth' box or a 'bumpy' box. Challenge a friend or whānau member to see if they can identify the theme of your collection just by feel.

BEAD MAZE

A bead maze can be a great way to focus your mind. Using natural materials such as sticks, vines and shells adds extra textures, making these structures even nicer to interact with.

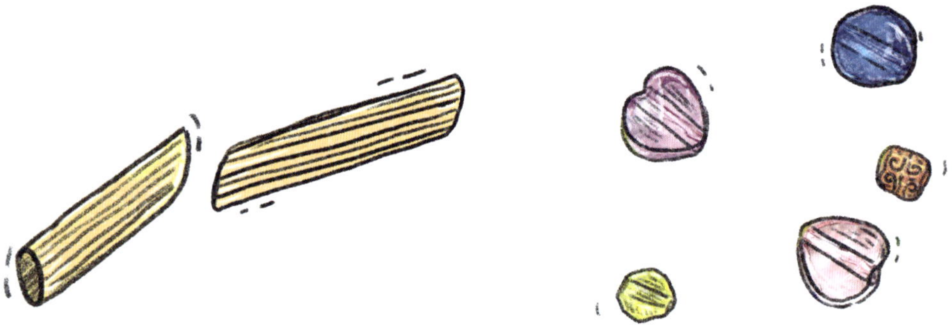

YOU WILL NEED:

Three to five long, thin, bendy sticks or vines – ivy, grape vine, willow and supplejack are all great plants to use

Soft ground or dirt to stick the vines into

Beads, pasta (tube shapes like penne or rigatoni), broken shells or anything you can loop onto the vines

WHAT TO DO:

1. Lay out your sticks or vines. Push the end of one of these into the ground.

2. Thread some of your beads, pasta and shells onto the stick or vine. Let the objects all fall to the ground.

3. Arc or loop the stick, being careful not to lift it out of the ground, and pierce the other end into the ground.

4. Repeat steps 1–3 for all your other sticks and vines. You could thread some of the vines through the loops of others so that you end up with an interesting tangled mess.

Spend some time moving the beads, pasta shapes and so on from one end of each stick to the other. Think about how you feel when you have moved the beads along each stick.

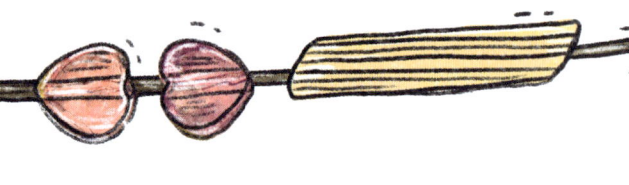

TIP
You could create your bead maze in a plant pot, so that you can move it around and use it for longer.

TIP
As with the 'Sensory box' activity on page 113, bead mazes are a great way to help young friends and whānau use their fingers and hands more confidently. Help a younger friend or whānau member to interact with your bead maze.

POWERFUL POSES – SHAPESHIFT LIKE MĀUI

The demigod Māui was a shapeshifter, able to take on the shapes of different animals.

Find a comfortable spot outside in your surroundings. Stand strong, take some deep breaths and hold a pose like:

A SLIPPERY TUNA/EEL

A SILENT TUATARA, LOW TO THE GROUND

A CHEEKY PĪWAKAWAKA/ FANTAIL THAT CAN QUICKLY FLIT AND STOP

A WHOOSHING KERERŪ, MOVING FROM TREE TO TREE TO EAT FRUIT

A STEALTHY, POWERFUL MANGŌ/SHARK

A MIGHTY MOA

How long can you hold each pose? Is it comfortable? Can you make other poses from nature? What animals can you copy? List them here.

_____
_____
_____
_____
_____

RHYTHMS OF NATURE

Sitting quietly, let your breath fall into a comfortable rhythm. What pace does your breath fall into? Is it fast or slow?

Now, listen to all the sounds around you. What can you hear? Music playing somewhere? Birds calling? Water dripping or flowing? The wind blowing? Are the sounds 'fast' or 'slow'? List what you heard here.

_____
_____
_____
_____
_____
_____

Try to match your breathing to a sound you can hear. How do you feel when you match your breathing to a 'fast' sound? How do you feel when you match your breathing to a 'slow' sound? Write your feelings down here.

_____
_____
_____
_____
_____
_____
_____
_____
_____

MAKE!

MINDFUL MANDALAS

The word mandala means 'circle'. A mandala is also a symmetrical pattern representing wholeness and life that some of the world's religions use to help focus the mind.

You can make a mandala in a number of ways, but a great way to work with nature is by using leaves or leaf prints.

YOU WILL NEED:

Lots of leaves - different shapes from different trees, but also quite a few of each kind of leaf

Petals - again, lots of different shapes but plenty of each kind

Rice, sand, dried beans, dried lentils (optional)

Piece of chalk

Flat ground to work on - concrete, tiles or wood are best, but you can still attempt this on grass or dirt or black paper

Piece of chalk

Paints and paintbrushes

Different kinds of leaves that you can use as 'stamps' (optional)

WHAT TO DO:

1. Find a spot on flat ground that you would like to work on, or lay out your paper if you are using paints. If you create your mandala on the ground, make sure it isn't anywhere people usually walk.

2. With chalk, lightly sketch your mandala design outline on the ground or on your paper. Start with a simple design like the one on the page opposite. Once you are happy with your design, go over the lines and make them thicker.

3. Choose the materials you will use to fill in your mandala design. If you are making your mandala on the ground, lay out leaves, flower petals, dried beans and so on in the different parts of your pattern, filling them in until no open spaces are left. If you are painting your mandala, remember that you can use things such as leaves as stamps to create really interesting patterns.

Once you've finished your first mandala, you might like to design a more complicated pattern. Do some research and find pictures of other mandalas for inspiration.

TIP
Start off with a small pattern the size of a dinner plate - you can make bigger, more adventurous mandalas as you get better at it.

IDEAS
Take inspiration from nature for your mandala design – think of a snowflake, a slice of kiwifruit or orange, or a spider web.

WONDERFUL WAI

Look at this image of Ngākuta Bay in the Marlborough Sounds for a couple of minutes. Notice the beautiful blue water. Imagine you are there. What does the water look like? What does the water feel like? What does it sound like? How do you feel? Why do you think the water makes you feel this way? Record your descriptions and observations below.

_____
_____
_____
_____
_____
_____
_____

Take photos or draw pictures of places with water and attach them to this page. Write down the name of the place and the date and time of day you were there. Look at your pictures from time to time and remember how you felt when you were there.

DRAW OR ATTACH HERE

WRITE!

OFF WANDERING ON AN ADVENTURE

In France, a flâneur is the word for a person who observes their surroundings – an urban explorer who wanders with little purpose other than to see what they might find or observe.

Give yourself some time to just wander. What do you observe? Do you see objects? People? Other living things? Try not to have a final destination in mind and see where you end up.

Use this space to take notes, draw pictures or add photos of what you see.

Date: _____

My wandering started here: _____

My wandering ended here: _____

It took this long: _____

People I saw: _____

_____
_____
_____
_____
_____
_____
_____
_____

BEWARE

It is safer to do this activity in an area with people around and not in the bush - unless you really know where you are going. Take an adult with you and a mobile phone. Wandering without a final destination in mind is great fun, but don't get lost!

Animals I saw: _____
_____
_____
_____
_____
_____
_____

Objects I saw: _____
_____
_____
_____
_____
_____
_____

Plants I noticed: _____
_____
_____
_____
_____
_____
_____

Sounds I heard: _____
_____
_____
_____
_____
_____
_____

Please circle one of these: It was warm/cold/windy/raining.

IT IS...

Find a spot outside to sit comfortably.

Think how you could finish these sentences:

The sky is _____

The ground is _____

I can smell _____

I can feel _____

I can hear _____

The _____ looks hard

The _____ looks soft

That _____ looks rough

That _____ looks smooth

The _____ looks hot

The _____ looks cold

The _____ looks wet

The _____ looks dry

I was suprised by _____

I was scared by _____

I felt happy looking at _____

NATURAL OVERLAP

In mātauranga Māori, or Māori knowledge, the presence of some things in nature are signs that other things are happening too. For example, when the pōhutukawa trees are flowering (in November and December), kina are ripe to harvest from the sea.

Choose a location that you can visit a few times over a year – ideally every three months so that you can see it in summer, autumn, winter and spring.

Sit quietly in this location and observe what is happening around you. Look specifically for things that happen at the same time or coincide. For example, what else is happening at the same time that daffodils or blossoms come out? Or when the trees drop their leaves? Write down what you have observed.

_____

_____

_____

_____

_____

_____

_____

_____

_____

_____

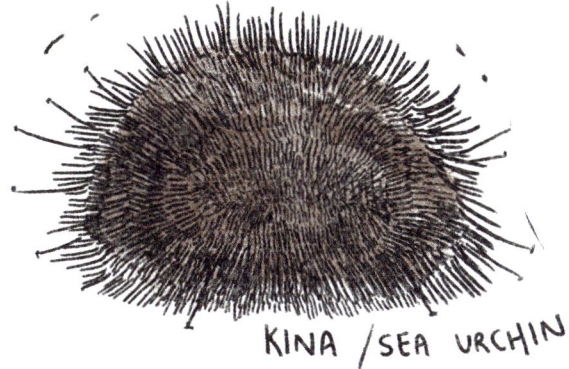

POHUTUKAWA

KINA / SEA URCHIN

TIP
Think about completing this activity at the same time as the 'A year of change' activity on page 32.

EVIDENCE OF ENERGY

Energy makes things happen. It can make things (including us) warmer, make things move, make things grow, light things up, cook our food and much more. There are lots of different types of energy.

Energy is all around us, and we can detect some of the effects of it using our senses – sight, touch, smell, hearing and taste. Even if we can't see a lot of energy, sometimes we can see the effect energy has on other objects.

Find a nice spot to sit comfortably. Look all around you. Focus on one thing that is happening and that you can see, hear or feel, like the leaves moving on a tree. Try to tune out everything else and focus on this one thing.

WHAT TYPE OF ENERGY ARE YOU SENSING? IS IT:

SOUND ENERGY

This energy moves in waves, but not ones we can see. We hear it as sound.

I sensed: _____
_____
_____
_____

LIGHT ENERGY

This energy also travels in waves. We see it as light (it is the only type of energy that can be seen).

I sensed: _____
_____
_____
_____

MECHANICAL ENERGY

This is the energy of something in motion. We see it in the form of a flowing river, a moving car, or a person jumping up and down.

I sensed: _____
_____
_____
_____

THERMAL ENERGY

This is also called heat energy. We feel it as heat.

I sensed: _____
_____
_____
_____

THERE ARE ALSO OTHER TYPES OF ENERGY:

CHEMICAL ENERGY

Nearly everything in the universe is made up of tiny particles called 'atoms', which join together to form bigger 'molecules'. Chemical energy is stored in the bonds that glue atoms together in molecules. This means that things like food, petrol and natural gas have lots of chemical energy just waiting to be used.

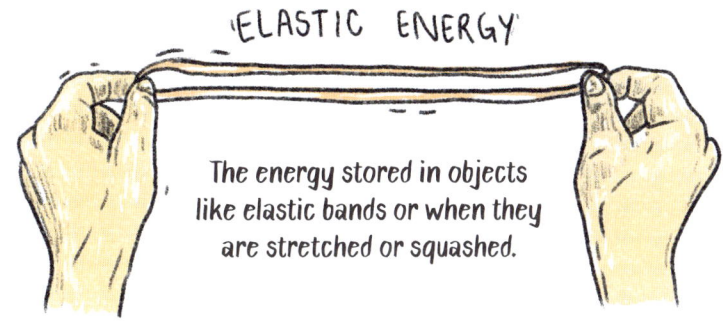

ELASTIC ENERGY

The energy stored in objects like elastic bands or when they are stretched or squashed.

ELECTRICAL ENERGY

We use a lot of this energy in our daily lives. Electricity is carried along wires and cables by electrons – tiny particles of energy. Lightning is another kind of electrical energy, which we can see as light energy and hear as sound energy when it causes thunder.

NUCLEAR ENERGY

The centre, or core, of an atom (see 'Chemical energy' above) contains energy. This energy is released when atoms join together (fusion) or split apart (fission). The sun is constantly undergoing fusion of tiny atoms, creating huge amounts of energy that living things on Earth benefit from.

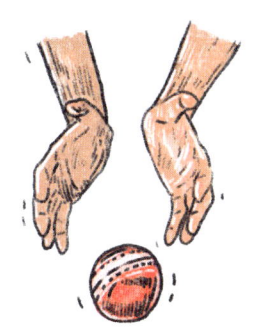

GRAVITATIONAL ENERGY

The energy an object has in relation to gravity. An object has more gravitational energy when it is higher off the ground.

RADIANT ENERGY

This energy moves in waves and includes energy from the sun, X-rays and radio waves. It is also called electromagnetic energy.

ENERGY EXPANDED

In the activity 'Evidence of energy' on page 126, you read about some of the different types of energy. But there are only two forms of energy – potential energy and kinetic energy.

POTENTIAL ENERGY

This is the energy stored in an object. Think about:

- A book sitting on a table – it has potential energy but hasn't been bumped off the table and fallen onto the ground yet.
- A battery – it has potential energy but hasn't been put into your toy yet to make it go.

KINETIC ENERGY

This is the energy an object has when it is moving. Think about:

- A book that got bumped off a table – it has kinetic energy while it is falling to the floor.
- A battery that has been put into the toy – it has kinetic energy now the tiny electrical charges it releases are moving around the wires in the toy, making the toy work.

SIT COMFORTABLY IN ANOTHER SPOT AND CONSIDER POTENTIAL AND KINETIC ENERGY. ASK YOURSELF THE FOLLOWING QUESTIONS:

What form of energy does a moving car have?

_____

What form of energy does a tree have? (Hint: think about how we use wood as fuel.)

_____

What form of energy does a bee buzzing around a flower have?

_____

What form of energy does the nectar in the flower have?

_____

Can you see a river flowing or waves on the ocean? What form of energy do these have?

_____

What form of energy does a parked car have?

_____

KŌWHAI

ACTION AND KAITIAKITANGA

ACTION FOR THE SIX Rs

There are a number of useful ways to reduce the number of things we buy, use and waste. The diagram below describes the 'Six Rs' – six ways you can have a more positive impact on nature and the environment.

Brainstorm some ways that you can put the six Rs into practice.

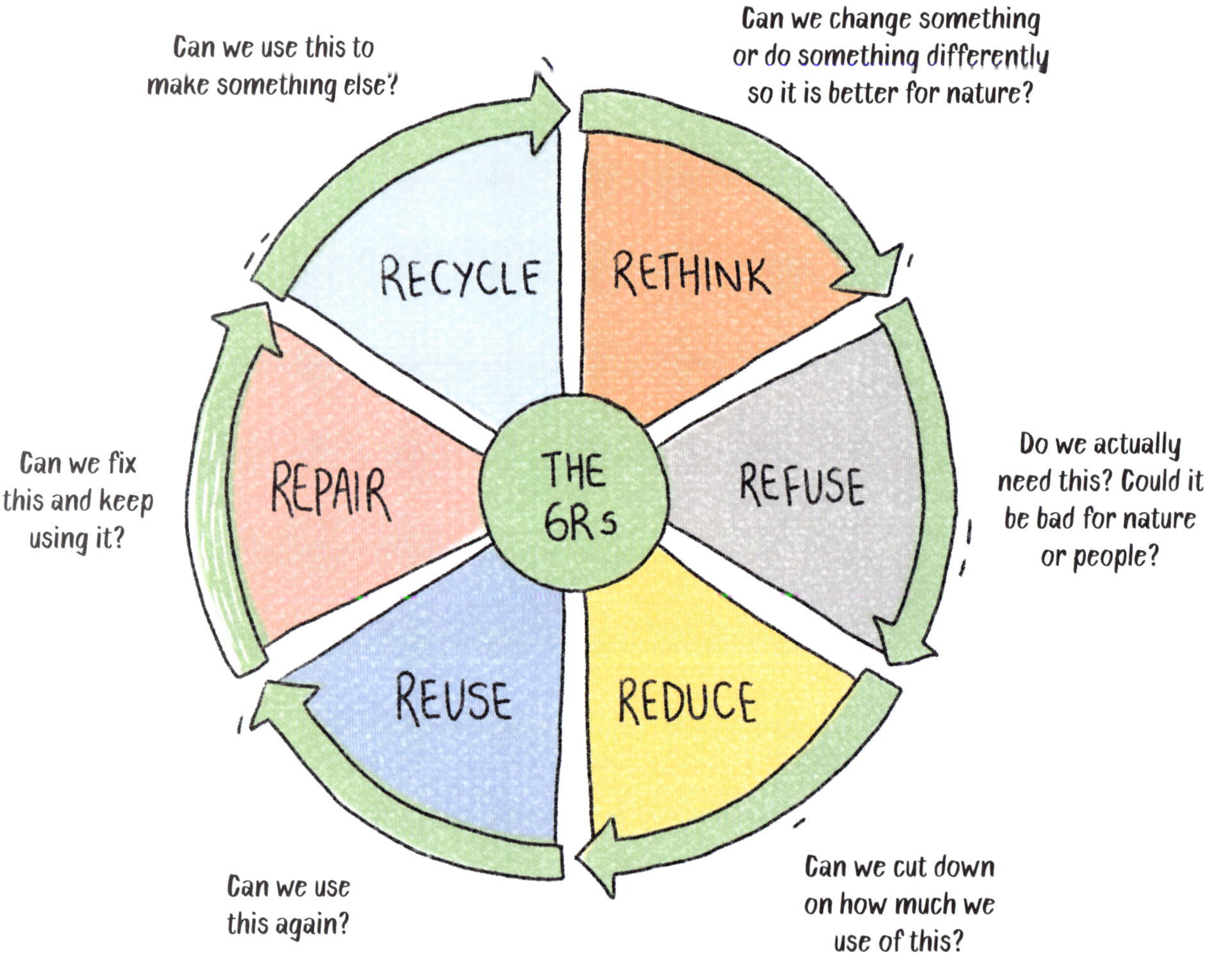

THE 6Rs

- **RECYCLE** — Can we use this to make something else?
- **RETHINK** — Can we change something or do something differently so it is better for nature?
- **REFUSE** — Do we actually need this? Could it be bad for nature or people?
- **REDUCE** — Can we cut down on how much we use of this?
- **REUSE** — Can we use this again?
- **REPAIR** — Can we fix this and keep using it?

CHALLENGE
Tag a friend (physically, or via text, email or social media) after you have completed an environmental action and get them to do the same – or better!

LITTER – WHAT'S THE REAL PROBLEM?

If you haven't already done so, complete the activity 'What does your house put into landfill?' on page 86.

What is the most common type of rubbish that your whānau throws out?

Can you come up with any ideas about how you and your whānau could reduce the amount of this rubbish you produce?

MOST COMMON RUBBISH

WHAT WE COULD DO INSTEAD

SUPERMARKET CHALLENGE

How much extra waste do you think your family buys without even noticing?

When you and your whānau next visit the supermarket, challenge yourselves to buy less waste by following this checklist:

- ☐ Choose items made or grown in Aotearoa New Zealand – that means less carbon was used to get it to the shop.

- ☐ Look for type 1 or type 2 plastics – these are the only plastics that can be commonly recycled in Aotearoa New Zealand.

- ☐ Buy large bags of chips, biscuits, dried fruit or nuts instead of single-serve or multi-packs. (You can use small containers to take a serving to school or work.)

- ☐ Buy bars of soap in paper packaging rather than plastic bottles of hand soap or body wash.

- ☐ Take reusable bags to bring fruit and vegetables, snacks and pantry staples home in.

Write down what you decided not to buy and what you bought instead.

WE DIDN'T BUY	WE DID BUY

T-SHIRT BAGS

You can recycle old tops by turning them into fantastic bags. They make great gifts to give to friends and family.

MATERIALS

Old T-shirt or tank top (singlet)

Scissors

WHAT TO DO:

1. (If you are using a tank top, you will not need to do this first step.) Making sure your T-shirt is the right way out, lay it flat on a table or the floor and fold it in half lengthwise. The sleeves should now be lying on top of each other. Cut off both the sleeves together along the seams. You will now be left with what looks like a tank top.

2. Cut out the neck of the shirt in a deep 'U' shape, leaving the shoulder straps on the top as these will form the handles of your bag.

3. Turn the shirt inside out and lay it out flat again, making sure the bottom edges line up evenly and there are no creases. About 2cm in from one of the sides of the shirt, use your scissors to cut a slit 10cm up from the bottom through both layers of the shirt (ask an adult for help if you need it).

4. Move along 2cm and cut another 10cm slit. Repeat this step until the entire bottom 10cm of the shirt is in strips.

5. Take the first strips of both the top and bottom layers and tie them together in a simple but firm knot. Repeat this for all the strips, making sure to tie the top layer to its bottom partner. The entire bottom edge should be a row of knots.

6. Take the first strip of the top layer and tie it to the second strip of the bottom layer. The first strip of the bottom layer will now be hanging by itself – just leave it there.

7. Take the second strip of the top layer and tie it to the third strip of the bottom layer. Carry on in this way until all the strips have been knotted to a different 'partner'. Note that when you get to the end, the final strip of the top layer will be left on its own like the first strip of the bottom layer – again, leave it there.

8. For the final knots, take the first two strips at one end of the bag and tie them together in a firm double knot. Repeat all the way along the bag until all the strips have been double-knotted.

9. Turn the bag the right side out and admire your creation!

1.

2.
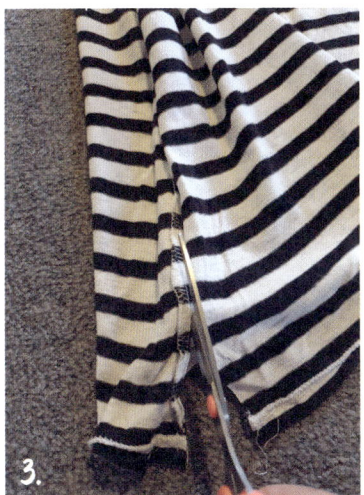
3.

4.

5.

6-8.

9.

137

MAKE!

NO-WASTE WALK

Organise a walk for your friends and whānau. This could be a flâneur-type adventure as in the 'Off wandering on an adventure' activity on page 122, or a specific walk you would like to do.

Challenge your group to pack a lunch or snacks that have no/very little rubbish or waste. If they need help, encourage them to:

- Pack fresh fruit such as grapes, bananas, apples or mandarins, or dried fruit like apricots, raisins or sultanas (put these in a container and avoid multi-packs).
- Pack sandwiches in a container or bag that can be washed and reused.
- Pack chips from a single large bag in a reusable container.
- Pack homemade biscuits or muffins (baked without paper wrappers).

WHAT DID YOU TAKE FOR LUNCH?

DID YOU PRODUCE ANY WASTE?

MAKE!

NO MORE PAPER TOWELS

Sometimes we use single-use items such as paper towels or napkins without really thinking about it. These items can be handy, but they can be easily replaced with reusable alternatives like cloth. You can make cloth napkins and then simply wash them and use them again and again.

YOU WILL NEED:

Clean old clothing (like shirts or T-shirts), sheets or towels

A ruler

Scissors (or pinking shears to prevent your napkins fraying)

WHAT TO DO:

1. Lay your item out on a flat surface.
2. Using your scissors, cut out squares measuring approximately 30cm by 30cm.
3. If you have used scissors rather than pinking shears, ask someone to sew a neat hem along the edges of your napkins – or ask them to teach you how to do this yourself.
4. Use these cloth napkins instead of paper towels, wash them when you're done, and reuse!

PAPER BAG CHALLENGE

Do you know how much rubbish or waste that you, on your own, produce in a day? What different kinds of rubbish do you produce? Is it mostly compostable plant waste? Is it recyclable waste? Or does it go into landfill?

Your challenge is to collect all the rubbish you produce over a day. It doesn't matter whether you're at home or at school. Are you up to it? (Please note that this does not include used toilet paper!)

To collect all your rubbish, you first need to make a paper bag.

YOU WILL NEED:
Double page of a large newspaper

Flat surface to work on

WHAT TO DO:

1. Open out your double page of newspaper and lay it out on a flat surface.
2. Fold up 5cm of the paper along the short edge and crease it neatly. You should have a crisp folded edge.
3. Flip the whole double page over, so that the folded edge is closest to you.
4. Fold the left side of the paper two-thirds of the way over to the right. Make a neat crease along the fold.
5. Fold the remaining third of the paper in from the right edge to the left. Make a neat crease along the edge.
6. Open up this last third of the page and lift up the first folded edge (only) of the paper underneath (the 'left' side from step 4). Tuck the third of the paper under this folded edge.
7. Flip the whole paper over again. Fold the top of the page down to the very bottom (where the folded edge is) and crease the fold neatly.
8. Tuck the top edge of the page under the folded edge at the bottom.
9. You have made a paper bag! Open it from the top (folded-over) edge.

Carry your bag around with you all day and use it to collect any rubbish you produce. This could be banana skins, wrappers, tissues, waste paper and so on.

How much rubbish did you produce? A little, some or a lot? Did the amount surprise you? What is your 'worst' waste (the waste you make most of)?

Can you think of any ways you could reduce this waste or deal with it better? For example, if you are putting lots of fruit waste in the rubbish bin, could you compost it instead? Write your thoughts here.

_____

_____

_____

_____

_____

_____

COMPACT COMPOSTING

If you have never tried composting but would like to give it a go, this is an easy way to start. It's also a great way to watch how composting works, as you can see the waste through the clear sides of the plastic bottle.

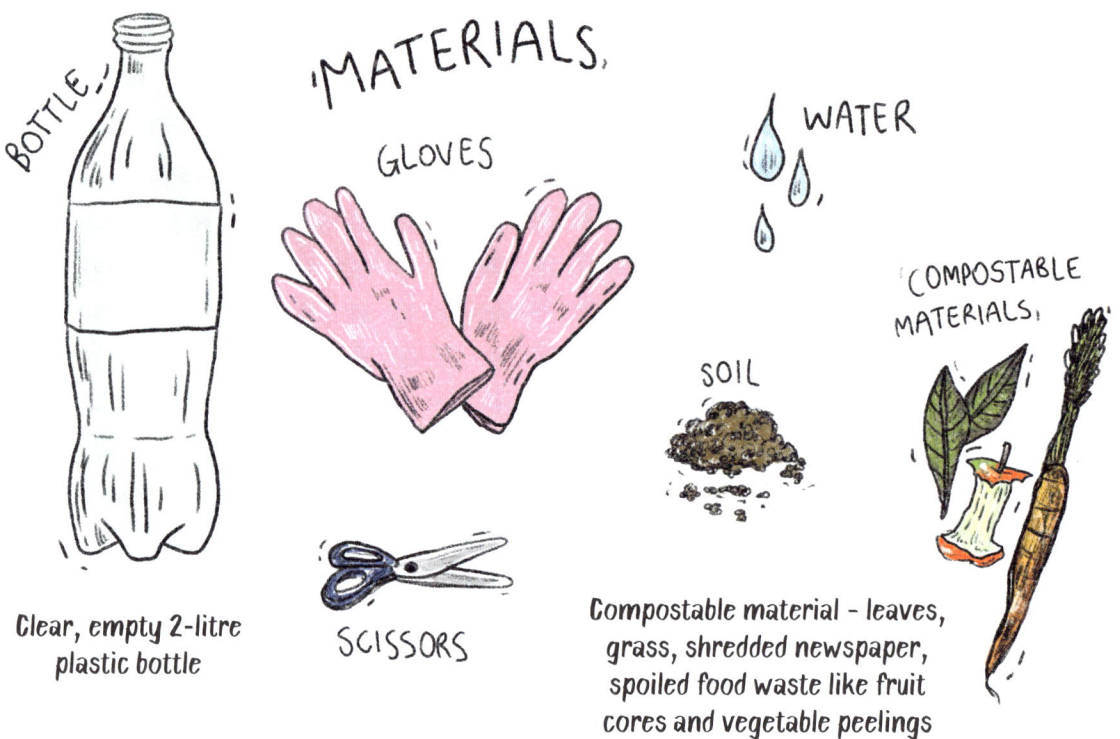

Clear, empty 2-litre plastic bottle

Compostable material – leaves, grass, shredded newspaper, spoiled food waste like fruit cores and vegetable peelings

WHAT TO DO:

1. Cut the top off the plastic bottle, leaving as much of the bottle as you can, and rinse it out well with water. Make sure you remove any labels so that you can see inside the bottle.

2. Put on your gloves and add a 3cm-deep layer of soil to the bottom of the bottle.

3. Add roughly a 2cm layer of your compostable material.

4. Alternate the layers of soil and compostable material until the bottle is full, leaving a 3cm gap at the top.

5. Add water. The soil and compostable material should be damp all the way through but not sitting in water, so add a little at a time and stop if you see water sitting in the bottom (you can gently tip out any excess).

6. Put the bottle in a sunny spot where it won't tip over and leave it to sit.

Check the bottle over several weeks and watch the compostable material break down. Add a little more water if it looks dry, but only enough to keep it damp. Your compost is ready to add to the garden when all the material has broken down into small bits that look and smell like fresh soil.

CHALLENGE

Look to see whether different compostable materials take longer to break down – for example, carrot or potato peelings. Check whether moving the compost into the shade affects how long it takes for things to break down. Is shade or sun better for the compost?

SIMPLE REUSABLE WRAPS

Reusable food wraps (sometimes called beeswax wraps) are an awesome alternative to using plastic cling film or foil.

These beeswax wraps are great for wrapping biscuits, fruit, vegetables and sandwiches (but not sandwiches with fish or meat fillings), and also for covering jars and bowls. Beeswax has natural antibacterial properties, making the wraps safe to use and stopping the growth of some germs.

YOU WILL NEED:

Ruler or tape measure

Scissors or pinking shears

100% cotton fabric in a design you like – the size is up to you (see the suggested wrap sizes on page 146 to work out how much fabric you'll need)

Baking paper

Iron and ironing board (and an adult to help you)

Organic beeswax pellets – roughly ¼ cup for a 30cm by 30cm wrap

Tongs

WHAT TO DO:

1. Using scissors or pinking shears, cut your fabric to the size you want (pinking shears give a zigzag edge that won't fray).

2. Cut two pieces of baking paper that are at least 5cm longer on all sides than your piece of fabric.

3. Place one piece of the baking paper on the ironing board and put the piece of fabric on top.

4. Sprinkle wax pellets or grated wax over the fabric, then place the second piece of baking paper on top.

5. Set the iron at the cotton setting and switch it on. (It needs to be hot enough to melt the wax but not so hot that it burns the baking paper.)

6. Iron over the paper so that the wax beneath it melts into the fabric.

7. Peel back the top layer of paper, pick up the fabric with the tongs and hold it in the air to dry – this happens very quickly!

8. If you missed any areas on your wrap, repeat the process, sprinkling wax over the bits that need it.

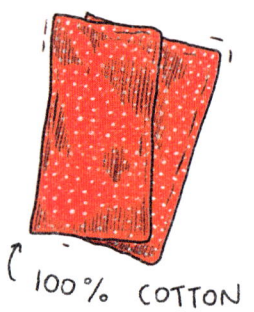

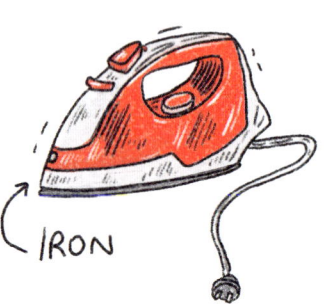
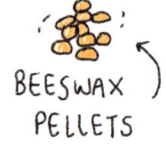

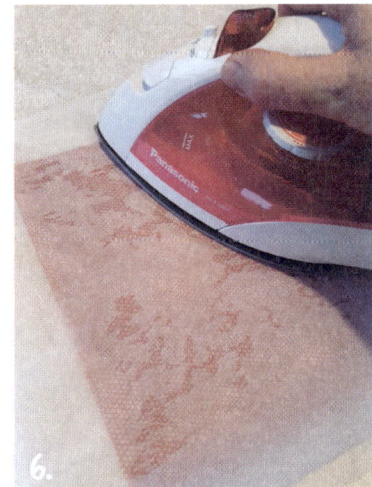
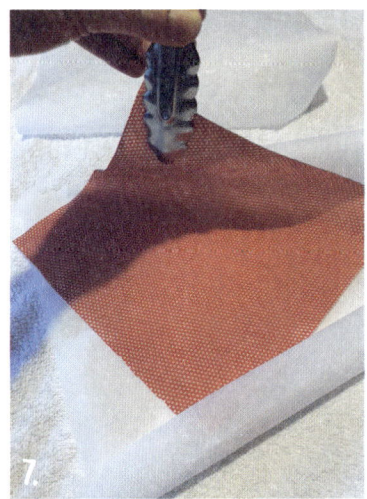

HOW TO CARE FOR YOUR WRAPS:

- Your wraps can be used in the fridge or freezer.

- Your wraps can't be used to wrap 'wet' foods, hot or warm foods, or fish or meat.

- Your wraps can be washed gently in cool water with eco-friendly soap and left to air-dry.

- Your wraps can last between a few months to a year, depending on use and care, and they can be renewed by rewaxing.

- Your wraps are made of cotton and beeswax, which are natural products. This means that when you have eventually finished using them you can put them in your compost bin.

MAKE!

DELUXE REUSABLE WRAPS

This method uses a few more ingredients than the 'Simple reusable wraps' activity on page 144, and thanks to the jojoba oil the wraps have more antibacterial properties. It takes about half an hour to make a few wraps.

YOU WILL NEED:

Ruler or tape measure

Scissors or pinking shears

100% cotton fabric in a design you like (see the table at right for suggested wrap sizes and ingredient quantities)

Oven

Baking tray

Baking paper

Saucepan

Water

Glass jug (this needs to fit inside the saucepan)

Powdered food-grade pine rosin*

Organic beeswax pellets*

Wooden spoon

Jojoba oil* (you could also try olive oil or coconut oil)

Paintbrush (use a new one, not an old painting one)

Wire rack

SMALL SQUARE WRAP (20 × 20cm)	MEDIUM SQUARE WRAP (30 × 30cm)
Good for snacks - cookies, fruit	Good for a sandwich
2 teaspoons beeswax pellets 2 teaspoons powdered pine rosin ½ teaspoon jojoba oil	4 teaspoons beeswax pellets 4 teaspoons powdered pine rosin 1 teaspoon jojoba oil

LARGE SQUARE WRAP (35 × 35cm)	CIRCULAR WRAP (40cm diameter)
Good for covering a bowl or plate	Good for covering a bowl or plate
5½ teaspoons beeswax pellets 5½ teaspoons powdered pine rosin 2½ teaspoons jojoba oil	5½ teaspoons beeswax pellets 5½ teaspoons powdered pine rosin 2½ teaspoons jojoba oil

WHAT TO DO:

1. Cut your fabric to size following the instructions for the 'Simple reusable wraps' activity on page 144 and the table above.

2. Preheat the oven to 110°C.

3. Line a baking tray with baking paper.

4. Half-fill the saucepan with water and bring to the boil.

5. Put the pine rosin in the glass jug. Place the jug in the saucepan (taking care the water doesn't overflow into it), turn the heat to medium and wait for the rosin to melt (this might take some time).

6. Once the rosin has melted, add the beeswax.

7. Using the wooden spoon, stir the mixture until the rosin and wax are completely melted and mixed.

8. Turn the heat to low and slowly drizzle in the jojoba oil.

9. Place one of your pieces of cotton fabric onto the baking paper.

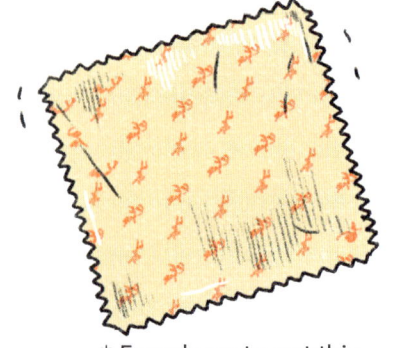

* For where to get this, see page 171.

TIP
In cooler weather you will need to warm the wraps up slightly in your hands before you can mould them as you want.

Staple a scrap of the fabric you used to make your wraps to this page.

10. Using the paintbrush, brush the fabric all over with the beeswax mixture (be careful, as the mixture and jug will be hot).

11. Place the baking tray in the oven just long enough (about a couple of minutes) to fully melt the beeswax into the fabric.

12. Take the tray out of the oven and paint more of the wax mixture onto the fabric with the paintbrush. Make sure the whole piece is coated evenly.

13. Lay another piece of cotton fabric (the same size or bigger) on top of the first piece to soak up the extra wax.

14. Turn both pieces over so that the 'soaking' piece is now on the bottom.

15. Return the baking tray to the oven just long enough for the wax to melt into the fabric.

16. Remove the tray from the oven and hang your first piece of wax-coated cotton on a wire rack to dry.

17. Use the paintbrush to spread more wax mixture onto the 'soaking' piece, which is now the next wrap to make. Repeat all the steps for as many cotton pieces as you have. The wraps are ready to use as soon as they are dry.

18. Use your wrap.

REPURPOSED POTS AND PLANTERS

Collect any containers you think might make great pots or planters. Think about how you might like to decorate these and where you might put them. If you want to put them outside, you'll need to make sure you use paints or glues that can withstand sun, rain and other weather conditions.

YOU WILL NEED:

Old cans (make sure the edges are not sharp), 2-litre plastic bottles, large yoghurt containers, glass jars (ask an adult to make some drainage holes in containers where this is possible)

Scissors

Warm, soapy water

Paints (use outdoor-paint test pots)

Paintbrushes

Shells, stones, beads and small tiles

Rope or twine

Exterior PVA glue

Gardening gloves or rubber gloves

Soil or potting mix

Spoon or trowel

Plants or seedlings

Water

WHAT TO DO:

1. Select the recycled container you wish to use as your pot or planter.

2. If you are using a plastic bottle, cut the top off using scissors (ask an adult for help if you need it). Cut the bottle at the height you want for your pot.

3. Wash your container in warm, soapy water and leave it to dry completely.

4. Gather together your decorating materials. You may wish to paint your pot one colour or in a multi-coloured design. You could also glue shells, stones, beads or tiles on your pot with exterior PVA. Or you could cover the outside surface of your pot with exterior PVA and then wrap rope or twine around it to cover it. It's entirely up to you! Once you've finished, leave the pot to dry.

5. Once your pot is completely dry, put on your gloves and fill it three-quarters full with soil or potting mix (see the note on page 155 for guidance on using potting mix).

6. Using a spoon or trowel, dig out a hole in the middle of the soil in the pot that is big enough to fit your plant or seedling.

7. Shake the excess dirt off the roots of your plant or seedling, then place it in the hole. Put more soil around the plant so its roots are well covered. Press the soil gently but firmly around the base of the plant.

8. Water your plant and place it in a location that's right for it – for example, does it need sun or shade? Now admire your beautiful work!

TIMELY TUCKER

Different fruits and vegetables naturally grow and ripen at particular times of the year. For example, asparagus can be found in spring; strawberries, oranges and apples ripen in summer; pumpkins are ready in autumn; and kiwifruit can be found in winter.

Some farmers do grow fruit and vegetables outside of their usual seasons so that they are available in supermarkets year-round, but this uses up lots more energy. Think about trying to grow summer fruits in the middle of a cold winter – you would have to grow them inside, and they would need lots of heat and light. Sometimes those fruits and vegetables are grown overseas in summer and brought to New Zealand for us to buy in our winter.

SO, WHAT SHOULD WE BE EATING AND WHEN?

When you are at the supermarket, a greengrocer's or a fruit and vegetable market, look to see what is being grown in Aotearoa New Zealand at particular times of year. Write down what you find:

Summer: _____

Autumn: _____

Winter: _____

Spring: _____

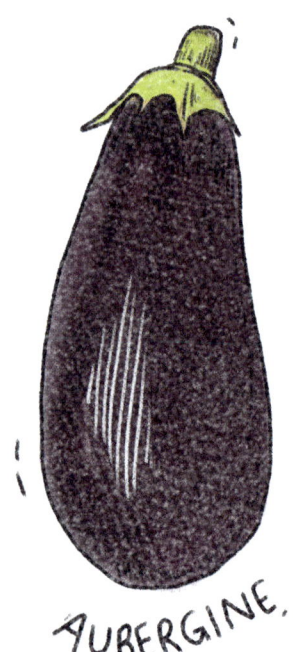

AUBERGINE.

What does this tell you about the kinds of foods you should be eating at different times of the year?

What season is it now? Can you think of some meals you could make with the locally grown fruits and vegetables that are available in your supermarket now? From your ideas, choose one and make it for your whānau (if you need help, ask an adult).

Season: _____

Meal ideas: _____

_____

_____

_____

_____

Write down the recipe (your own or one you have found) and draw a picture or take a photo of what you created.

Recipe: _____

_____

_____

_____

_____

_____

_____

_____

_____

NECTARINE.

BROCCOLI.

MARAMATAKA AND KAI

Maramataka is the Māori lunar calendar. It names particular times of the year when different types of food are traditionally planted, collected and stored. What can you find out about each of these times of the year? When are they and what activity is done in each?

Poutūterangi: _____

_____

Kohitātea: _____

_____

Haratua: _____

_____

Māori gave each night of the lunar month its own name. Particular nights are considered better or worse for planting and fishing. What can you find out about these nights of the month? When are they and what activity is done in each?

Turu: _____

_____

Ari-roa: _____

_____

Ōrongonui: _____

_____

Māwharu: _____

_____

Traditional Māori practices that show kaitiakitanga (guardianship and conservation) include: placing temporary bans (rāhui) on taking food from an area – for example, at times of year when animals are breeding; using the lunar calendar to decide when to plant and when to harvest; taking only what is needed so there is no waste; and hunting and fishing only for food, not for sport – respect for wildlife is important.

NOTE
Different iwi have different traditions relating to the nights of the moon. Those above are adapted from Ngāti Kahungunu.

MAKE!

A PLATE OF PLANT POWER

Eating more plant-based meals is good for the environment and can be great for our health (plants are full of vitamins and minerals).

Find a vegetarian or vegan dinner you can make that impresses your whole whānau.

Write down the recipe below and share it with a friend. Challenge them to make some plant-based plates of their own and swap recipes.

INGREDIENTS:

WHAT TO DO:

draw here!

MAKE!

EGG-CARTON SEEDLINGS

You can grow seedlings in egg-carton cups using the seeds you collect from fruits or vegetables.

WHAT TO DO:

1. Using scissors, cut the egg carton into individual egg 'cups' (you may need an adult to help as this can be tricky).

2. Moisten each egg cup with water.

3. Put on your gloves and use a spoon or trowel to fill each cup with some potting mix or soil to about 1cm below the top edge.

4. Place the seeds on top of the soil. If you have cherry tomatoes, it's great fun to squeeze and pop the seeds into the soil! For small seeds like these and chilli or capsicum seeds, you could plant four or five in each egg cup. For larger seeds like beans, just put one in each cup.

5. Scatter some more soil thinly on top so the seeds are covered.

6. Place all the egg cups onto the plate or waterproof dish, making sure each cup sits flat on the surface.

7. Water your seeds by pouring water onto the plate or dish (so the cups can soak it up). Place the egg cups in a bright, warm spot, but not necessarily in direct sunlight – an inside windowsill can be a good spot.

8. When the seedling has grown two to four true leaves, it can be planted straight into your garden. To do this, simply take the seedling and egg cup and plant the whole thing straight in the ground in your desired spot – the egg cup will eventually rot away. Or you may choose to plant the seedling in a larger container on a windowsill in a sunny spot. Make sure you water your seedling when you plant it out, and keep watering it regularly.

How did your plant turn out?

YOU WILL NEED:

Scissors

Cardboard/paper egg carton (one that takes a dozen eggs)

Water

Gardening gloves or rubber gloves

Spoon or trowel

Potting mix or soil

Seeds from fresh tomatoes (cherry tomatoes are great), chillies, capsicums or beans

Plate or waterproof dish (the egg-carton cups need to sit flat on this)

IMPORTANT

Before you use potting mix, get an adult to help you and make sure you follow these guidelines for health and safety:

- Make sure you wear gloves when handling soil, compost or potting mix.
- When you open a bag of potting mix, open it slowly and point the opening away from your face.
- If you are in an inside space, make sure it is well ventilated.
- If the mix is dry, wet the soil before using it to reduce dust.
- After working with potting mix, wash your hands carefully before eating, drinking or putting your hands anywhere near your face.
- For more information, check out the WorkSafe New Zealand website.

TIP

You can plant your seedlings into the pots you make in the 'Repurposed pots and planters' activity on page 149.

ATTRACTING BIRDS

The native birds of Aotearoa New Zealand are beautiful companions and need our help. Over winter, it can be really difficult for birds to find food. We can help them by planting trees, shrubs and other plants that have winter flowers and berries. Even if they aren't already your neighbours, birds like tūī, korimako (bellbirds) and kererū can travel long distances to find flowers and fruit – you never know who might turn up!

Even if you don't have a garden, small plants and shrubs placed in pots on balconies or out the front of buildings will encourage wildlife. If you need help, ask a local garden centre for some advice on what plants to choose.

Kākā, korimako (bellbirds), tauhou (silvereyes) and tūī all eat nectar, fruit and insects. Kererū eat fruit, some leaves, and new growth from plants.

FOR FRUIT AND SEEDS

- Kanono or raurēkau (*Coprosma grandifolia*)
- Karaka (*Corynocarpus laevigatus*)
- Karamū (*Coprosma robusta*)
- Kōtukutuku/tree fuchsia (*Fuchsia excorticata*)
- Makomako/wineberry (*Aristotelia serrata*)
- Mingimingi (*Leucopogon fasciculatus*)
- Nīkau palm (*Rhopalostylis sapida*)
- Pūriri (*Vitex lucens*)
- Shiny karamū (*Coprosma lucida*)
- Tī kōuka/cabbage tree (*Cordyline australis*)

FOR NECTAR

- Harakeke/flax (*Phormium tenax*)
- Houhere/lacebark (*Hoheria populnea*)
- Kōtukutuku/tree fuchsia (*Fuchsia excorticata*)
- Kōwhai (*Sophora* species)
- Pōhutukawa (*Metrosideros excelsa*)
- Pūriri (*Vitex lucens*)
- Rewarewa/New Zealand honeysuckle (*Knightia excelsa*)
- Tī kōuka/cabbage tree (*Cordyline australis*)

RIORIO

KANONO

Plant some native plants, then keep a record of which birds come to visit when they flower or fruit.

DATE	BIRD	PLANT

MAKE!

HOMEMADE BIRD TREATS

You can make bird treats to support your feathered friends over winter, or even just to encourage them to feed in a spot where you can watch them.

HOMEMADE BIRD MIX

YOU WILL NEED:

Equal parts of the following:

Sunflower seeds (hulls still on)

White millet

Shelled peanuts

Cracked corn

Dried fruit – raisins, currants, sultanas

WHAT TO DO:

1. Mix all the ingredients together in a bowl.
2. Place the mix in a bird feeder or on a dish or surface outside that is out of reach of predators like cats.

HANGING FRUIT FEEDER

YOU WILL NEED:

Homemade bird mix (see above)

An apple or orange

Sharp knife (ask an adult for help)

Spoon

2 bamboo skewers

4 × 20cm pieces of string or twine

WHAT TO DO:

1. Cut your apple or orange in half.
2. Using the spoon, scoop the flesh of the fruit out to make a fruit feeder bowl.
3. Pierce a skewer through the fruit skin, about 1cm under the rim of your fruit feeder. Push it through to the opposite side, so the bowl is in the middle of the skewer.
4. Repeat step three, but on the other side – the two skewers should form an 'X' shape, with the fruit feeder bowl in the middle.
5. Tie one piece of string to the end of each skewer, and go outside and find a sturdy branch, away from cats and other predators, to tie your fruit feeder on to.
6. Loop the strings around the branch and tie them together so that the feeder hangs flat. Scoop your homemade bird mix into the feed bowl.

Now watch for the birds to land and feed! What birds did you see? Check your feeder every few days and top it up with the extra bird mix.

TIP

For more ideas for bird feeders, see the 'Attracting birds' activity on page 156.

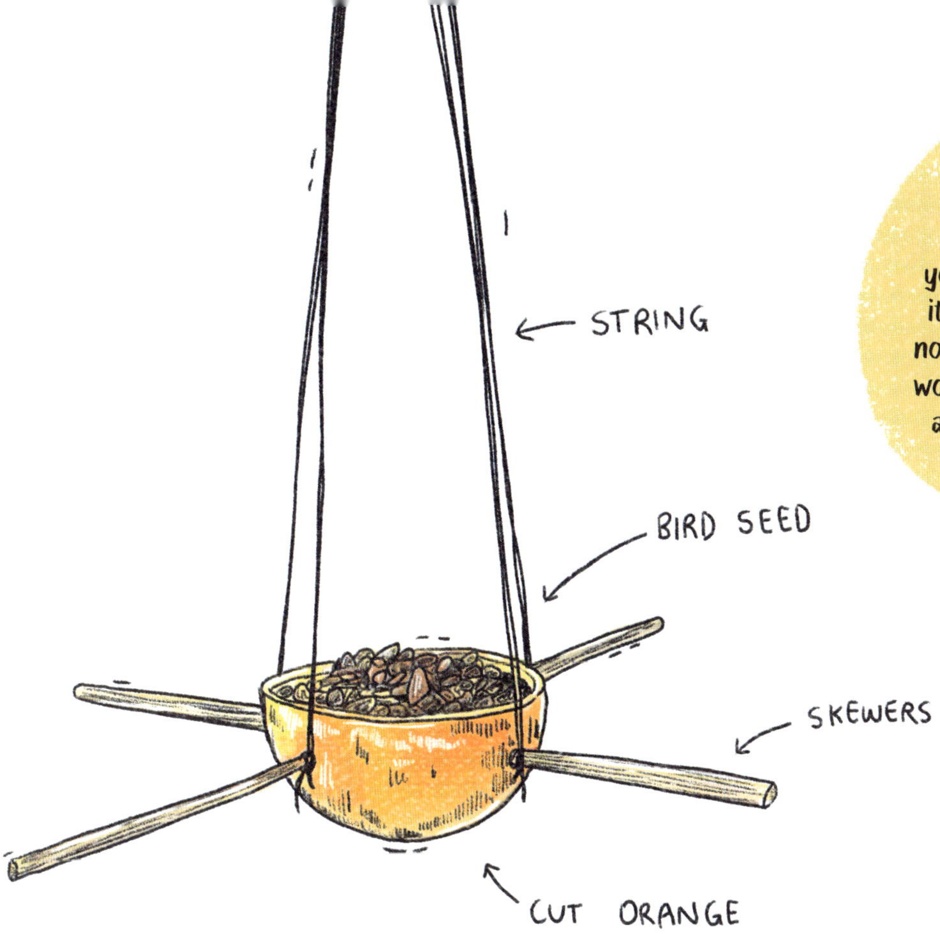

← STRING

← BIRD SEED

← SKEWERS

← CUT ORANGE

NOTE
If this is the first time you've fed birds in your garden, it may take a while for them to notice that the food is there. They won't be used to your house being a feeding spot and it may take a little time for them to arrive and feed.

MAKE!

BUG HOTELS AND BEE B&Bs

Did you know that Aotearoa New Zealand has 28 species of native bee? These are not the bumblebees or honeybees we know very well, but much smaller bees that don't live in hives or sting like honeybees but do like to pollinate our native plants.

Most of our native bees nest in the ground, but yellow-masked bees (*Hylaeus* species) make their homes in hollow twigs and branches. These bees are very small (not quite a centimetre in length) and are mostly black with yellow markings on their face, chest and back. We can help our native bees flourish by making bug hotels, or bee B&Bs, for them to live in.

Bug hotels are homemade homes for insects. They come in a wide range of types and sizes to support different kinds of insects. The hotels provide the insects with a space to rest, nest and hibernate (sleep) over winter, and offer them protection and shelter.

The instructions on the opposite page will help you make a bug hotel that is suitable for insects like the bees and ladybirds that are native to Aotearoa New Zealand.

KEY TIPS FOR MAKING A BUG HOTEL:

- Small is good – you don't really want to host a whole minibeast zoo, especially if some of the neighbours might try to eat one another. Instead, try a small bug hotel first and aim to make it a good home for just one or two types of insects.

- Go natural – make your bug hotel from natural products that don't contain any chemicals like dyes, paints or bleaches. Where you can, consider using recycled materials.

- Keep them clean – make sure there is no mould growing on your hotel that might hurt your insects. Check it occasionally to ensure it is clean.

- If you build a bug hotel for bees, make sure it is located near flowers and plants so the insects have a good food source nearby. Make sure no plants are growing in front of the hotel and blocking the insects from coming and going. Place the hotel in a spot that is sheltered from wind and rain, but in the sun so that it gets nice and warm.

CHALLENGE

For more elaborate models and for more information on the bees native to Aotearoa New Zealand, check out the websites on page 171.

YOU WILL NEED:

Recycled 2-litre plastic bottles

Scissors

Empty toilet-paper rolls (or paper towel rolls cut into three sections)

At least twenty to thirty lengths of thin bamboo (about 4-5mm across in diameter)

WHAT TO DO:

1. Using scissors, cut the bamboo canes so each piece is the same length as the toilet-paper roll (ask an adult for help if you need it). Cut them so that one end is closed (cut after the 'node' section in the bamboo) or the whole length is hollow (so you can blow through it like a straw).

2. Making sure the hollow, open ends of the bamboo are all facing outwards at one end, slide the pieces of bamboo into the toilet-paper roll. Keep putting more bamboo lengths in until they are packed tightly and won't fall out. This is your bug hotel.

3. Cut the plastic bottles in half lengthways, so you end up with what looks like two long dishes (again, ask an adult for help if you need it). You will need one half-bottle for each hotel you make.

4. Place your bug hotel in a warm, quiet spot in a tree or bush no higher than 1m off the ground. Make sure it is nearly level, with the open ends of bamboo slightly lower so that any water can flow out of the tube if needed.

5. Tuck in the half-bottle securely above and over the toilet-paper roll (you could even let it curl around the toilet roll – but not too tightly).

NOTE

The best time to make and put out native bee hotels is in spring. The best time to make and put out ladybird hotels is in early autumn (April-May) so the insects have somewhere to hibernate (sleep) over the winter. You may even want to bring your ladybird hotel into a spot like a garden shed (not the house) during winter to protect the sleeping bugs from cold and rainy weather. You can take it back outside to the same spot in spring.

MAKE!

MAKE YOUR OWN PAPER

Making your own paper from old, used paper is really satisfying. There are photos of most of the steps to help you.

WHAT TO DO:

Make the frame

1. Cover a flat surface with an old tablecloth.
2. Take one of the picture frames and lay it on your work surface, 'front' side up, with no backing or glass.
3. Cut a piece of mesh/netting that is about the size of the frame (ask an adult for help if you need it).
4. Lay the mesh so that it covers the whole frame, to the edges. Use nails or staples to fix one side of the mesh in place. Make sure the mesh is really flat and taut as this will form the shape of your paper, then fix it to the frame on all the other sides (this is called the 'mould'). Cover any sharp edges of the mesh or staples with duct tape so that the mould is safer to handle.
5. Leave the second frame as it is, without mesh or netting (this is called the 'deckle'). If needed, cover any sharp edges with duct tape so that the deckle is safer to handle.

Make the paper pulp

6. Shred all your paper and soak it in water overnight.
7. Put some shredded paper in a blender, add lots of water (more than the amount of paper) and blend it until you can't see any clumps of paper or unshredded paper. This is your paper pulp.
8. Put the paper pulp into the large tub.
9. Repeat steps 6–8 until you have enough paper pulp to fill your tub to a depth of about 10cm.

Make your paper

10. Spray one of the old blanket (or jumper) pieces with water.
11. Hold the two frames facing each other so that the mould is on the bottom with the netted ('front') side facing up, and the deckle is on the top with the smooth ('front') side facing down.

YOU WILL NEED:

Old tablecloth to cover your work space

Two identical picture frames

Scissors

Mesh or netting, like that used on window insect screens

Nails and/or staples

Hammer

Duct tape

Used paper - preferably used computer paper (old newspaper will give you a darker colour and poorer-quality paper)

Water

Food blender to mash up the paper

Large tub or sink that can fit both frames lying down (one on top of the other)

Spray bottle filled with water

Old wool, acrylic or polyester blanket or old jumper, cut into rectangles that are the same size as your frames (you will need as many rectangles as the number of sheets of paper you want to make)

Sponge

Heavy books to press the paper

12. Keeping the frames together, submerse them fully in the tub of paper pulp. Now rock the frames back and forth in the tub (still holding them flat together) so that the pulp is evenly distributed over the mesh.

13. Quickly lift up both frames. The pulp will be stuck to the mesh of the mould. Hold the frames above the pulp and let the extra water drip off for about ten seconds.

14. Move the frames to your work surface and remove the deckle. There will be no pulp where the deckle was.

15. Place a piece of old blanket on top of the mould, over the pulp.

16. Holding the edges of the blanket piece against the edge of the mould, flip the entire thing over so that the mould is now flat on the blanket with the pulp facing down.

17. Gently press the sponge down on the mesh to soak up excess water from the pulp.

18. Slowly lift up the mould. The paper pulp will stay lying on the blanket.

19. Use your mould and deckle to make another piece of paper (repeat steps 10–18). As you make each piece of paper on each piece of blanket, lay it on top of the others so that you have a big stack. If you make lots of sheets of paper, you may need to add more pulp to the tub.

20. When you have made enough pieces of paper, place one more piece of blanket on top of your stack and then put some heavy books on top of that.

21. Wait two or three hours, then lift off the books. Lay out each piece of blanket and paper sheet one by one to dry. Your paper should be dry and ready to use after about a day.

Use your paper to make some birthday or Christmas cards, or write a letter to a friend. Cut a piece of your paper to stick onto the page opposite, too.

14.

15.

16.

17.

18.

TIP
Use the dyes you made in the 'Nature's dyes' activity on page 74 to colour your paper, and/or cut it into any shape you like.

"Stick" YOUR PAPER HERE →

FINDING OUT MORE

GLOSSARY

Absorption — The process of taking in or sucking or swallowing up something such as a liquid in a natural or gradual way.

Atom — The smallest part of a substance that can exist.

Classify — Arrange things into groups or categories according to similarities or shared features.

Compass — An instrument containing a magnetised pointer that shows the direction of magnetic north and bearings from it (e.g. south, west and east).

Compost — Decayed organic material used as a fertiliser for growing plants.

Deciduous — Trees that lose their leaves every year (as opposed to 'evergreen' trees, which keep their leaves year-round).

Deity — A god or goddess.

Density — The degree of compactness of a substance. For example, if an object is heavy and compact, it has a high density, or is 'very dense'.

Energy — Having the ability to 'do work', causing things to change and move.

Environment — The natural world.

Evidence — Facts or information indicating whether something is true or valid.

Experiment — A scientific procedure undertaken to make a discovery, test an idea or demonstrate a known fact.

Force — A push or pull upon an object resulting from its interaction with another object.

Habitat — The natural home or environment of an animal, plant or other living thing.

Inorganic — Not from living matter.

Insect — An invertebrate that has a body made up of three sections, with six legs (three pairs) and usually one or two pairs of wings. Insects include beetles, wasps and bees.

Invertebrate — An animal lacking a backbone. Also called 'minibeasts'.

Kaitiakitanga	Traditional Māori practices that show guardianship, conservation and stewardship.	
Kapua	A cloud or bank of clouds.	
Landfill	Getting rid of rubbish by burying it.	
Litter	Rubbish or waste.	
Maramataka	The Māori lunar calendar, an important guide used to decide activities such as when to plant and to harvest crops, and when to go fishing.	
Mātauranga Māori	The body of knowledge originating from Māori ancestors, including the Māori world view and perspectives, and Māori creativity and cultural practices.	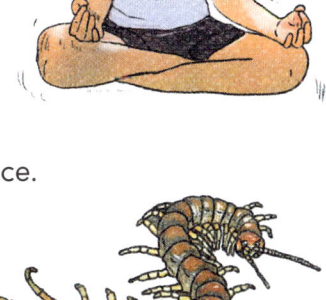
Materials	The matter from which an object is or can be made; also the things needed for the activities in this book.	
Mindful	Focusing awareness on the present moment.	
Mineral	A solid, naturally occurring inorganic substance.	
Minibeast	See 'Invertebrate'.	
Molecule	A group of atoms bonded together.	
Mythical	Occurring in, or characteristic of, myths or folk tales.	
Native	An animal or plant that comes from, or occurs naturally in, a particular place.	
Observation	Closely monitoring something or someone.	
Organic	From living matter.	
Papatūānuku	Earth mother.	
Pattern	A repeated design.	
Personification	The representation of a thing or idea as a person.	
Pollution	Something that has harmful or poisonous effects and is present in, or has been added to, the environment.	
Predator	An animal that naturally preys on (hunts and eats) other animals.	
Prediction	Making a guess or forecasting what will happen.	

Ranginui	Sky father.
Recycle	Convert waste into reusable material.
Reduce	Make smaller or less in amount or size; use less of something.
Reflection	An image seen in a mirror or shiny surface.
Refuse	Another word for litter or rubbish.
Repair	To fix something or restore it to a good condition.
Research	To study or investigate something.
Resources	Supplies or materials used for certain purposes.
Rethink	Consider something again.
Reuse	Use again or more than once.
Rock	A natural material made up of specific minerals.
Sediment	Little bits (particles) of rocks, minerals, sand, fossils and other matter that can be carried and deposited by water, ice or wind.
Seedling	A young plant.
Sensory	Relating to the physical senses of sight, smell, touch, hearing or taste.
Species	A group of living things in which the individuals are similar and can reproduce (have babies).
Symmetry	Having two halves that are the same.
Tamariki	Children.
Taniwha	Mystical creatures seen by Māori as part of the natural environment.
Tāwhirimātea	The Māori god of the weather. His parents were Ranginui and Papatūānuku.
Te ao Māori	The Māori world or Māori world view.
Texture	The way something feels when you touch it.
Three-dimensional	(3D) Having or appearing to have length, width and depth.
Two-dimensional	(2D) Having or appearing to have length and breadth (width) but no depth.
Wai	Water.
Whānau	Extended family or family group.

WEBSITES

Bumblebee Conservation Trust
www.bumblebeeconservation.org/bee-nest-boxes
A brief guide to bee nest boxes.

Department of Conservation (DOC)
www.doc.govt.nz
Search 'day hikes gear list' for DOC's recommended gear list for day walks.

For the love of bees
www.fortheloveofbees.co.nz/native-bees
Information on the native bees of Aotearoa New Zealand and how to help them.

Meat Free Monday
www.meatfreemonday.org.nz
This organisation helps you with ways to cut back on eating meat to help the environment.

Mother Nature Network
www.mnn.com
Search 'hotel wild bees' for a resource for building bee hotels.

New Zealand Plant Conservation Network
http://www.nzpcn.org.nz
Search 'deciduous plants in New Zealand' for a list of plants that are native to Aotearoa New Zealand.

Open Air Laboratories
www.opalexplorenature.org/Beehotels#/0
A resource for building bee hotels.

Physics Classroom
www.physicsclassroom.com
Search 'force' for an explanation of the meaning of force.

Pure Nature
www.purenature.co.nz
This Aotearoa New Zealand company supplies the ingredients needed to make the reusable wraps on pages 144 and 146.

Royal Society for the Protection of Birds (RSPB)
www.rspb.org.uk
Search 'build a bee bomb' for the RSPB's guide to building a bee B&B.

Te Ara
www.teara.govt.nz/maramataka-the-lunar-calendar
This web page has a lot of helpful information on maramataka, the Māori lunar calendar.

www.teara.govt.nz/tawhirimatea-the-weather/
Head here for more information about Tāwhirimātea and the weather.

www.teara.govt.nz/wasps-and-bees/page-4
Information on the native bees of Aotearoa New Zealand.

THANK YOU

ACKNOWLEDGEMENTS

This book is for my daughter, Isla, and my ever-supportive husband, Todd. You make life a constant adventure, for which I am grateful every day.

I am also grateful to my parents, Jos and Arnie, who made family adventures the norm from when I was very young, and my brother, Chay, who I tried to keep up with (it was more like chasing at times!).

Thank you to inspirational environmentalists and scientists such as David Attenborough, Carl Sagan, Jane Goodall and Dian Fossey, who graced our TV screens back in the days when our family sat together watching documentary shows on Sunday evenings, looking at each other in awe and marvelling at what was out in the world. That was a precious time in my childhood.

A big thank you to Nicola Legat at Te Papa Press and Pamela Streeter at Te Papa for their support and motivation, and for giving me the opportunity to write this book. I am also grateful to Pippa Keel for her amazing illustrations, Kate Barraclough for her graphic design, Brad Haami for his advice on mātauranga Māori, Susi Bailey and Mike Wagg for editing the book and Estelle Best for managing the project.

Rachel Haydon, August 2020

ABOUT THE AUTHOR

Rachel Haydon is a qualified primary school teacher and scientist with a Bachelor's degree in Zoology and a Master's in Marine Science. She has more than 15 years' experience of teaching science to children of all ages in schools, museums, zoos and aquariums in Australia, South Korea, the United Kingdom and Aotearoa New Zealand. She has been lucky enough to work at the Natural History Museum (London), the Zoological Society of London, the Museum of New Zealand Te Papa Tongarewa and the National Aquarium of New Zealand.

Rachel is committed to motivating children of all ages to get outside and explore, and to enjoy and protect the natural world and all that lives within it.

ABOUT THE ILLUSTRATOR

Pippa Keel is an award-winning illustration designer, who has an Honours degree in illustration and a huge love of the outdoors. From her small studio in Wellington, Pippa has worked with a variety of New Zealand-based companies and publishers, including Zealandia Ecosanctuary and the Museum of New Zealand Te Papa Tongarewa. Getting outside into nature to camp, tramp and explore has been a part of Pippa's life since before she could walk, so she was stoked to help create this book and encourage others to do the same.

First published in New Zealand in 2020 by Te Papa Press
PO Box 467, Wellington, New Zealand
www.tepapapress.co.nz

Text © Rachel Haydon
Illustrations by Pippa Keel, © Museum of New Zealand Te Papa Tongarewa.
Photographs © Rachel Haydon, except for: **29** AI.033257, Te Papa (Jean-Claude Stahl); M.138236, Te Papa (Norman Heke); FE012955, Te Papa (Maarten Holl); SP104402, Te Papa (Carlos Lehnebach); **46** 2016-0008-54, Te Papa (Maarten Holl); **62** 1999-0003-1, Te Papa (Michael Hall); **67** CT.014344, Te Papa (Melissa Irving); **96** (upper right) James St John, CC BY 2.0; (lower left) Titus Tscharntke; **120** Daniel Stockman, CC BY-SA 2.0.

This book is copyright. Apart from any fair dealing for the purpose of private study, research, criticism, or review, as permitted under the Copyright Act, no part of this book may be reproduced by any process, stored in a retrieval system, or transmitted in any form, without the prior permission of the Museum of New Zealand Te Papa Tongarewa.

TE PAPA® is the trademark of the
Museum of New Zealand Te Papa Tongarewa
Te Papa Press is an imprint of the
Museum of New Zealand Te Papa Tongarewa

A catalogue record is available from the National Library of New Zealand

ISBN: 978-0-9951136-8-8

Design by Kate Barraclough
Illustrations by Pippa Keel
Digital imaging by Jeremy Glyde
Printed by 1010 Printing Asia Ltd